Better Homes and G

Biggest
Book of
De ve
ng

BIGGEST BOOK OF DECORATIVE PAINTING
Editors: Paula Marshall
Project Manager: Carol Linnan
Contributing Editor: Cathy Long, Carol Linnan
Graphic Designer: Craig Hanken, Heather Von Arb, Studio P2
Copy Chief: Terri Fredrickson
Publishing Operations Manager: Karen Schirm
Senior Editor, Asset and Information Manager: Phillip Morgan
Edit and Design Production Coordinator: Mary Lee Gavin
Editorial Assistant: Kaye Chabot
Book Production Managers: Pam Kvitne, Marjorie J. Schenkelberg, Rick von Holdt, Mark Weaver
Contributing Proofreaders: Becky Danley
Indexer: Bev Nightenhelser

Meredith® Books
Executive Director, Editorial: Gregory H. Kayko
Executive Director, Design: Matt Strelecki
Managing Editor: Amy Tincher-Durik
Senior Editor/Group Manager: Vicki Leigh Ingham
Marketing Product Manager: Tyler Woods

Publisher and Editor in Chief: James D. Blume
Editorial Director: Linda Raglan Cunningham
Executive Director, New Business Development: Todd M. Davis
Executive Director, Sales: Ken Zagor
Director, Operations: George A. Susral
Director, Production: Douglas M. Johnston
Director, Marketing: Amy Nichols
Business Director: Jim Leonard

Vice President and General Manager: Douglas J. Guendel

Better Homes and Gardens® Magazine
Editor in Chief: Karol DeWulf Nickell
Deputy Editor, Home Design: Oma Blaise Ford

Meredith Publishing Group
President: Jack Griffin
Executive Vice President: Bob Mate

Meredith Corporation
Chairman and Chief Executive Officer: William T. Kerr
President and Chief Operating Officer: Stephen M. Lacy

In Memoriam: E.T. Meredith III (1933-2003)

contents

introduction

More and more people are turning to decorative painting when attempting to create a beautiful home. Color scheme, pattern, and texture all play a unique role when beginning this sometimes overwhelming task.

The use of decorative painting will simply enhance and enrich each room—at an economical cost—allowing your own individuality and creativity to stand out. Imagine at the end of this journey, the dull walls of your home being enlivened, furniture and floors transformed with splendid color and patterns, and boring accessories refreshed with lively motifs.

Before beginning this task, peruse through the whole house tours in Chapter 2, featuring three different homes, and see how the homeowners planned their very different interiors around decorative finishes. Learn their secrets about how to tastefully incorporate multiple finishes. Each chapter thereafter will help you to create a color palette from your own personal preferences, lifestyle, and real-life possessions. With the help of decorative painting techniques, and tips and advice from experts, each room will come alive with warmth and personality. If you still aren't sure what works for you, take the Discovering Your Inner Hue quiz on page 59. Or, if you question how the orientation, location, siting, and features of your home affect choices, see the Whose Hue to Use? checklist on pages 62–63.

Whether it is a living room, dining room, bedroom, or bathroom that is a challenge, decorative painting and painted furniture are smart ways to beautify and transform a room. Budget-friendly, unfinished, or dated pieces of furniture can grace the most fashionable set-tings. Painted furniture also mixes well with stained wood and upholstered furnishings to pull an entire room's look together.

To experience the decorating potential of painted furniture and the medley of settings and ideas for living and dining areas, bedrooms and baths, children's rooms and nurseries, and outdoor spaces, look through each individual chapter for tips and techniques.

Featured rooms will give you ideas on painting methods, stenciling, and stamping projects. Step-by-step instructions for decorative painting techniques, pages 232–318, will provide you with the tools to accomplish the look and style you desire and more—allowing you the joy of artistic expression.

Discover the use of stencils and stamps, and learn how to make a few of your own. These methods allow you the freedom to choose the patterns and colors you love—whether you decorate your whole house, a room, a wall, or a single piece of furniture.

Remember, color is one of the constants in our lives. From earliest childhood, we all have natural color preferences, favorite colors that warm our lives and soothe our souls. Colors lift our moods or remind us of pleasant memories. We can create our own environments based on the colors that make us happy. Whatever your color passions turn out to be, you'll find dozens of examples throughout this book. So, surround yourself and fill your home with the colors you love.

Checkerboard Patterns

Striped Walls

Painted Paneling

Sponging Techniques

Faux-Tiled Walls

instant color

PAINT AND THE BASICS OF COLOR. If you know what color or colors of paint you want to use in a room, great. With today's technology, paint stores can mix and tint to match whatever shade you love. Just about anything works—a swatch of fabric, a piece of porcelain, artwork, a photograph, even a chambray shirt.

WHEN YOU HAVEN'T DECIDED ON THE SHADE YOU WANT, START WITH THREE TO FIVE SAMPLES OF PAINT CHIPS IN YOUR COLOR RANGE. (More than five is generally confusing.) Some companies today offer oversize chips, which are easier to see than the smaller, multishade cards. Tack up the chips and observe the colors at different times of day and with artificial and natural light. When you have two or three shades that work, buy a pint of each and paint a wallboard scrap or wall section in your choice. If your room has varying light conditions, such as a wall of windows or French doors, paint sections in two or more spots to be sure you are happy with your choice. It's easy for even an experienced decorator to be fooled by the effects of light, floor coverings, and furnishings on paint colors. So unless you are absolutely certain of your choice, don't skip this step.

Remember, too, that the finish of the paint—flat, satin, eggshell, semigloss, or gloss—will affect the light-reflecting qualities and the ultimate color. What finish you choose is a personal preference, although flat paint is generally preferred for less-than-perfect walls. Paint

with some shine, such as satin or even shinier semigloss, is also used in kitchens, baths, or children's rooms, as it's easier to scrub. Again, depending on your preference, you might like the light-reflecting qualities of semigloss paint for a dramatic dining room used at night or even a small decorative powder room. Semigloss is used for woodwork and trim, but follow your taste.

- **Caution:** White and off-whites are at least as tricky as vivid colors. **One final tip:** *If you love a color, but it's overpowering, switch to a lighter value of the same paint chip. It's also possible to get the paint store to custom mix a shade between two adjacent values on the paint chip.*

HOW MUCH PAINT TO BUY?

Paint cans usually state the one-coat coverage you can expect from 1 gallon of paint or primer. For many paints, including primers, a gallon will cover about 400 square feet. But it's still a good idea to calculate coverage. Measure the perimeter of the room (all walls). Multiply the result by the ceiling height to get the square footage. Round off to the full foot. Don't deduct for windows or other openings unless they add up to more than 100 square feet. Divide that figure into the number of square feet that a gallon of paint promises to cover. Round up to the nearest whole number. Buy accurately, as it is difficult to match paint if you need more or to dispose of properly if you buy too much. However, it's always a good idea to save paint for touch-ups, especially if you think you may rearrange artwork or rehang window hardware.

WHAT OTHER SUPPLIES DO I NEED?

The tools are simple but necessary for interior painting. Here's what you will need for the basic paint jobs:

- *Primer*
- *Brown paper drop cloths for the floor; heavy plastic drop cloths for furniture*

- *Surfacing compound and knife to apply it, sandpaper, painter's tape, edger*
- *Metal paint pan, plastic liners, roller with threaded handle for extensions, sash and trim brushes. Most interior jobs call for a 7- or 9-inch roller frame. Use a long pole for the ceiling and a short pole (2 feet long) for walls.*

WHAT WALL PREPARATION IS NECESSARY?

A smooth, clean, dry, mildew-free wall does count. If your wall isn't in good condition, the prettiest paint color won't compensate. Before you even think about starting to paint, scrape or sand away rough spots. If necessary, strip old wallpaper. Depending on the paper and how it was applied, you may find a spray-on liquid combined with scoring to be less cumbersome than renting a steamer. If you do rent a steamer, follow the directions carefully to avoid accidents. If any glossy surfaces remain, dull them with sandpaper or liquid sandpaper. Scrub walls with mild detergent and water. Rinse with a sponge and clear water. For mold and mildew, wash with a solution of 1 quart household bleach and 3 quarts of water.

For the smoothest finish, always prime and treat spots with a special primer that prevents bleed-through. Don't ever paint over damp or wet walls. If the weather dampens the walls inside or out, run an air-conditioner or dehumidifier or wait for a dry day.

HOW DO THE PROS PAINT WALLS?

The best materials pay off in a professional-looking job. Purchase quality primers, paints, brushes, and rollers. A top-quality paint rolls on smoothly and evenly and has the depth of color lacking in some bargain paints. Latex paints are the norm today for most interior paint jobs. They are easy to apply, and brushes and rollers clean up with soap and water. However, because it's tough and durable, consider oil-based paint for kitchen or bath cabinets.

If you are using a synthetic roller cover, precondition it by rinsing with water and spinning dry. (Do not precondition a lamb's-wool roller.) Use a metal tray, with disposable plastic liners, as it's more stable than a paint can and can be attached to a ladder. Fill only one-third of the tray with paint. Load the roller by rolling it in the deeper end of the tray, then smoothing it on the sloping surface until the paint is distributed evenly. Paint the ceiling first, starting with a narrow strip at the ceiling line, then walls around openings and along the baseboards. Use a brush, edging roller, or paint pad for this; use a small brush or trim roller for corners.

When applying paint to large surfaces, make a letter M (3 feet across and 3 feet high), then fill in spaces, working from the unpainted area into the wet paint. If you are using the same paint for walls and woodwork, paint the woodwork as you get to it. If the woodwork will be another color, paint it after you have completed the walls.

SPECIAL CASES:
CHECKERBOARD FLOORS

Tape measure

Graph paper

Wood filler

Hand sander

Tack rags

Paint (two colors of oil-based enamel or floor paint)

Straightedge

Gray charcoal pencil

Chalk line

Quick-release masking tape (1½ inches wide)

Acrylic matte medium

Matte-finish, nonyellowing polyurethane

- **Measure** your room.
- **Transfer the measurements** to graph paper and chart out a check repeat that minimizes partial checks around the edges.
- **To prepare floor,** fill gaps with wood filler and sand smooth. To make the job

easier, rent a small hand sander for do-it-yourself projects. A commercial sander for floor refinishing is difficult to handle.

- **Pick up** sanding residue with a tack rag.
- **Paint the entire floor** in the lighter shade. Let dry.
- **Sand lightly.** Pick up sanding residue again with a tack rag.
- **Mark your pattern only** along the floor edges, using a straightedge and gray charcoal pencil.
- **Stretch a chalk line** across the room between the markings; snap lines to create the pattern.
- **Tape off darker squares** using 1½-inch-wide, quick-release masking tape.
- **Rub edges to secure** tape to the floor.
- **For a clean edge,** spread a light coat of acrylic matte medium available at art supply stores along the edge of the masking tape.
- **Paint the squares** with two coats of the darker color of your choice.
- **Allow adequate drying time** between coats. Seal with two coats of matte-finish, nonyellowing polyurethane.

SPECIAL CASES: STRIPED WALLS

Painter's masking tape for
    decorative painting
Carpenter's level
Measuring tape
Primer
Two shades latex wall paint
Pencil
Paintbrushes

- **Decide how wide** you want stripes (probably from 2 to 4 inches).
- **Prime walls** with a premium-bond primer. After they dry, paint on a base coat. Allow to dry to avoid smudging.
- **Measure and mark stripes** on the wall with a pencil, using the level to ensure straight lines. Don't erase or you'll smudge the wall.
- **Mask off every other stripe** with tape, as follows. Carefully mask the outer edge of each pencil mark with quality painter's masking tape. Tightly seal

down the edge next to the pencil lines with your fingers to prevent the paint from bleeding through. Test a small area first to be safe.

- **Paint the stripes of bare wall** exposed in between the masked-off stripes. Use smooth, even strokes.
- **After the color is applied,** gently remove the tape before the paint dries, being careful not to smear it.

SPECIAL CASES: SPONGING

Paintbrushes
Primer
Paint (two or more shades)
Natural sea sponges
Pie tin

- **Apply a primer or extra coat** of your base paint for a smooth finish.
- **Paint a solid base coat** and let dry overnight. Don't rush drying.
- **Test your technique** and color combination in a hidden place on a wall or on scrap board.
- **Wear disposable plastic gloves** instead of household rubber gloves, which leave fingerprint impressions. Change gloves as needed.
- **Use natural sea sponges** (not synthetic) to achieve a soft, mottled look. Vary the sizes for interesting effects.
- **Wet your sponge** with water, wringing it out thoroughly. This makes the paint adhere better to the sponge.
- **Pour a small amount of paint** into an old plate or pie tin and dip the sponge into it.
- **Cover the sponge** with a small amount of paint—too much will weigh it down. Blot excess with a newspaper.
- **Cup the sponge** in your hand and push lightly onto the surface. Practice first.
- **Space the patches of color** evenly, but change the position of the sponge for an irregular, mottled effect. Close, overlapping marks have a sleek look; widely spaced sponging with little or no overlap produces a casual appearance. Try spacing first, then fill in as you prefer.
- **To apply several layers of color,** dab

the first color over the base coat. Let it dry completely. Apply the second and third layers, drying in between.

SPECIAL CASES: PAINTING WOOD PANELING

Sandpaper and tack cloths
Paintbrushes
Liquid sandpaper
Shellac or clear lacquer
Alkyd primer
Latex paint

- **Sand paneling to remove** the gloss and wipe with tack cloths. Or apply liquid sandpaper, a deglossing agent.
- **Seal knots in paneling** with shellac or clear lacquer. Let dry completely.
- **Brush on an alkyd primer tinted** to match your paint color; allow to dry.
- **Apply one or two thin coats** of latex paint.

SPECIAL CASES: FAUX TILED WALL

Eggshell finish, off-white latex paint
Eggshell finish, white latex paint (quart)
Two shades of latex paint in your colors
Straightedge and level
Two small rollers
Small paintbrushes

- **Start** with a light, clean wall; paint off-white if necessary.
- **If wall is freshly painted,** allow to dry thoroughly. Using a straightedge, level, white paint, and small brush, freehand paint the mortar lines that will divide 4×4-inch tiles. (See page 251.) Paint the mortar lines freehand—don't tape—to keep the effect loose and casual. For easy spacing, start at center of each wall and work out.
- **Using a smaller roller** for each color, paint inside the mortar lines. While the paint is still wet, brush over each "tile," using separate brushes for each color.
- **Allow the painted wall** to dry thoroughly. Thin leftover off-white paint with acrylic urethane and brush over the walls for a color-washed effect.

◆ *above:* When your living and dining rooms flow into each other, think blending, but not necessarily identical color schemes. Here, the living room walls are a lighter shade of the taupe used in the adjoining dining room, handsomely framed by the cased opening. For visual harmony, trim color (or stain) and flooring should match when rooms open to each other.

◆ *right:* For an exact color match, roll up your rug and take it along to a paint store. Consider that colors look different on walls than on floors. To be safe, have a test pint mixed and paint a square before doing your room. You might want to go lighter or darker.

tried & true

Even if you are moving into a new house, it's unlikely you'll start totally from scratch when you choose your color palette and paint colors. Usually, you are working with some givens—a favorite painting, upholstered furniture, collections of pottery or plates, or as in the recently redecorated older home shown here, a handsome needlepoint rug. Pulling a wall color from a rug is a favorite tried-and-true decorator trick, as wall colors are easy to mix. And, shopping for a rug to match or blend with an existing wall color is notoriously difficult. Here, the homeowner took full advantage of the shades of taupe and black in a living room rug purchased for a previous house. For the color palette, three wall shades emerged that work well with existing furniture and art. The lighter taupe creates a serene background for collected furnishings and regional art in the living room. A darker shade of taupe, paired with slate black, gives instant drama to a previously small, drab dining room. The stylish two-tone effect emulates the look of wainscoting at the cost of a can of paint.

◆ *above:* Take advantage of an existing chair rail and enliven your dining room with two complementary colors. Contrast lighter and darker colors for drama. If you like a subtle look, choose two shades of the same color. To visually anchor the space, paint the darker color or shade below the chair rail to give the effect of painted wainscoting.

Turn to paint to transform flea market finds and unfinished buys into fashion furnishings.

a way of life

CREATE THE LIVING ROOM THAT FITS YOUR TASTE AND LIFESTYLE BY MIXING PAINTED FURNISHINGS TO SHOWCASE INEXPENSIVE FINDS. Look for furniture that is compatible in scale and spirit no matter what its style or era. For the easiest start, anchor your scheme with one or two focal pieces and work from there. Forget the maxim of small furniture in a small room. Pick a few larger tables or chairs. Feel free to mix new and old pieces with your own painted furniture creations. For interesting pieces that have discreetly peeling paint, brush away loose paint to avoid paint chips. If you have children in your home, seal such furniture with a matte polyurethane to avoid contact with old lead-based paint. (All new paints are lead-free.) Paint walls a vibrant color and add favorite collectibles from flea markets to design a welcoming living room and dining area.

◆ An overscaled architectural-salvage coffee table balances the painted metal daybed in this cottage living room and shows off its fashionably aged finish through the transparent glass on the tabletop. White paint freshens the flea market curved sewing cabinet and the crisp woodwork, providing contrast for the buttercup yellow and rich red painted walls.

◆ Floral fabrics in the slipcovered armchair, cushions, pillows, and balloon shades soften the room and add cottage appeal. The romantic setting is emphasized and personalized with a patterned rug, canine collectibles, and a vintage dollhouse.

LOOK FOR PAINTED PIECES TO FIT
YOUR SPACES. IF YOU CAN'T FIND THE
RIGHT PIECE, BROADEN YOUR SEARCH
TO INCLUDE UNFINISHED OR SECOND-
HAND FURNITURE TO PAINT AND
DETAIL TO YOUR OWN SPECIFICATIONS.
Accent pieces by local artists are an
interesting way to introduce painted
furniture into your home.

◆ *right:* Found at a California flea
market, a green armoire with peeling
paint fits a shallow wall in a small cottage.
The trio of miniature Adirondack chairs
serves as a reminder of summer fun.

◆ *below:* Stenciled cornflower blue
flowers adorn a vintage painted sewing
cabinet. Bright daisies provide an element
of surprise and the inspiration for the
fresh flower arrangement on this versatile
piece of furniture.

◆ *left and below left:* Yellow and red walls create an upbeat background for the metal table taped and painted by a local artist. Such bold color pairings energize rooms filled with white furniture or other neutral pieces.

◆ *top and left:* The harlequin-patterned accent table pairs a scrolled, bistro-style base with a taped-off and painted top. Coats of clear polyurethane ensure long wear and protect against scratches. The Eiffel Tower model, from a Paris flea market, dresses up the arrangement.

◆ *above:* New furniture crafted from salvaged components elevates vintage furniture to new heights. The coffee table shows off intricate detailing of the Victorian era. Peeling paint—overlaid with glass on the top—adds to the charm.

when textures enliven

By COMMON DECORATING DEFINITION, NEUTRAL SCHEMES TEND TO BE IN THE NATURAL SHADES OF OFF-WHITES, CREAMS, BEIGES, AND PALE TAUPE. These colors are close enough on the color wheel that it's fair to consider them monochromatic palettes. It comes down to this in decorating. How do you get the soothing quality of a neutral, basically one-color or no-color scheme and avoid boredom? When color isn't the key player, you use shapes, textures, and carefully chosen patterns for warmth and interest.

Start out easy. Think of your room with neutral walls and major furniture as your first decorating step. Begin easy with lamp bases in different materials—such as wrought iron and metal or wood. Nothing jarring, just different. Use the same approach with window treatments, chair seats, throws or accent pillows. Consider how accessories fit into the overall scheme without overpowering. Pottery, distressed tin, wooden accents—all introduce texture without color and pattern. Use architectural fragments, such as crown molding, subdued framed prints or a marbleized fireplace to enhance a room rather than bright paintings. Mix the smooth with the rough, the rustic and the refined—such as wooden accents softened with glass and pottery pieces for added interest.

◆ *opposite:* Textures— Because the ceilings are high (11 feet) in this living room space, white molding are added level with the window tops to even out the proportion and bring the eye down. Below the molding a light gray paint provides a neutral background for this country inspired room, while, above, a beige linen pattern on the walls adds visual interest and draws the eye toward the playful checkerboard design on the ceiling.
◆ *right:* A marbleized fireplace steps out in style, accenting the existing colors of the room's decor.

naturally harmonious

WORKING WITH COLOR IS PART ART AND PART SCIENCE, BUT THERE ARE SOME GIVENS THAT MAKE IT A LITTLE EASIER. You'll often hear the terms "value" and "intensity" used in referring to color. Value simply means how light or dark the color is. Blue, for example, can be a very pale pastel—a light value— or midnight—a dark value. Intensity means how clear or bright the color is. What can be confusing is that pastels (light values of colors) can also be bright. Hot pink may be pink, but it's certainly vivid. There are no right and no wrong color or value mixes. But when you choose colors of the same value and intensity, the effect is naturally harmonious. If you want your overall effect to be light and airy, without the drama of sharp contrast, choose equally pale shades of the dominant colors you are using. Pair a pale shell pink, for example, with a delicate apple green rather than a jewel-tone forest green. Or, if you lean to brights, plan your main scheme so the colors balance each other.

◆ *above:* Though colors are limited to shades of taupe and cream, the faux-painted screen, dark antique bed, and painted checkerboard floor create a contrasting, exciting scheme.

◆ *left:* When neutrality reigns, vary fabrics and finishes to avoid the beige blahs. Here the tone-on-tone bed hanging contrasts nicely with the diamond-patterned painted floor and the striped window seat cushions. The crisp white linens and shutters balance as serene solids.

COLOROPTIONS *Instead of noncolor neutrals, employ quiet shades of naturally soothing green, nature's calm-down color. Use greens alone or add accents of gray to turn down the volume as you mix subtle patterns.*

COLOR**OPTIONS**

◆ *above:* Consider how adjoining rooms relate to each other. For interesting variation in the living room, the greens and golden yellows are bleached (lightened). Melon is added to energize the mix. For the most versatility, keep your sofa neutral and introduce color with an armchair and accent pillows. The armchair fabric repeats as accent pillows. Repeat colors at least twice to tie the scheme together.

◆ *right:* As you introduce touches of color, experiment with adding textures and subtle patterns, too. For a quick accent, drape a soft throw over a sofa or chair. Or, introduce such details as the decoupaged lampshade, stacked, framed prints, and fresh flowers.

◆ *opposite:* Use creative touches, such as the drapery panels, to maximize small focuses of color. Interest comes from the scale and shapes.

COLOROPTIONS *Want more accent choices for neutrals? If you like colors that warm, consider these shades from orange to yellow-green.*

add pattern to palettes

EXPRESS YOUR COLOR PERSONALITY WITH LIVELY COMBINATIONS THAT SUIT BOTH YOUR DECORATING MOOD AND YOUR STYLE. For a quick start, begin with a focal-point fabric that has all the colors you plan to use. Then add at least two more patterns in varying scales. For harmony, repeat at least one of the colors from your focal-point fabric in the supporting fabrics or wallcovering. Or, for a more subtle mix, consider smaller scale fabrics that blend without repeating colors as the more formal example illustrates. The idea is for the shades and patterns to gently complement each other, without a dominant fabric. (Colors of the same brightness are easiest to mix.)

◆ *opposite:* With blue and red as the repeating colors, stripes mix pleasantly with a floral cotton and a two-color quilt. Employ accents, such as the checkerboard, to introduce another pattern and texture. For more pattern, add a blue-and white plaid or red-white-and-blue plaid fabric.

◆ *right:* Subtle mixes of pattern give interest without vivid color or large scale. Use the walls; here, layering pigment plaster on a wall truly gives it dimension. Select colors within the same family (for instance yellow and orange) for the most pleasing finished look. Implement splashes of color and add texture throughout the room like the floral centerpiece and lemon tree in the corner. Dressed in a modest stripe fabric, walnut stained chairs along with the oversized tablecloth, add pattern to the color palette and a bit of interest without a lot of intensity.

warmed by patterns

If you like the idea of neutrals in a live-lier scheme, vary patterns without distracting competing colors. In pleasing schemes, the lights and darks of a neutral color create the soothing palette. However, several shades of cream or taupe may be enough interest, especially if your plan is a quiet setting. Beyond painted floors, consider the less drastic step of a floorcloth in a traditional setting. Or, try woven fabrics or subtle stripes that offer interest without the focus of a strong pattern. As long as the shades are all variations of one color and the designs subtle, you can mix in a variety of patterns. Be careful how you combine textures to avoid the jarring contrast of rough with shiny.

◆ *top:* With a light, neutral background, American Colonial natural and painted wood pieces mix easily. The background also creates a gallerylike effect for the oil portrait above the mantel.

◆ *right:* Use a neutral scheme to update a mix of traditional-style furniture pieces. The restricted palette and muted prints allow the disparate styles to create a relaxed, yet sophisticated scheme that invites relaxation.

◆ *above* : Adding a warm faux wood look to a plain coffee table like this greatly increases its appeal. "Faking" wood is easier than it may seem. By gently blending light and medium warm tones together, rather than imitating true wood grains, you gain the effect without having to worry about trying to match any real wood species.

◆ *left*: The antiqued finish updates this reproduction French provincial-style table. The details of the table apron and legs readily absorb glaze for an ornate look. Reproduction furniture made after World War II is easily found at tag and garage sales as well as secondhand shops and thrift stores. Choose furniture pieces that are in good condition, that require a minimum of repairs, and that are not sealed with plastic-type laminates. **See page 287 for techniques.**

◆ *above* and *left:* A combination of taping and hand-painting results in energizing motifs for this stock unfinished armoire. You can either stencil or stamp similar motifs. Lively pieces work best in settings where they assume a starring role, as other furnishings become supporting players. Two cheerful primary colors enliven the setting—the bright red contrasting with the yellow-striped walls. **See page 287 for techniques.**

◆ *left:* Based on inlaid Moroccan mosaics, the painted tabletop transforms a basic budget-priced pedestal table into a memorable work of art. Intricate designs such as this enrich the setting. **See pages 290–291 for techniques.**

◆ *below:* A pair of antiqued reproduction French-style chairs share the painted mosaic table in a congenial grouping. The paisley fabric used to recover and update the chair seats and cushions enhances the rich color choices for the tabletop. Paisley and mosaic, merged with Asian-style pieces, offer a sophisticated and exotic setting in which the table becomes the focal point.

It's tempting to jump right in and start painting. Don't. You'll be happier with the results if you consider the size and scale of your room and your existing furnishings and patterns. **Begin by noting the ceiling heights, windows, and doors.** Then consider the size, placement, and patterns of your furniture. **Take everything into account before you decide on the scale of your painted pattern. Be particularly observant** when you are dealing with stripes, diamonds, or any of the repeated patterns. For example, wide stripes may fit the scale of a large room, but can overpower a child's tiny room. **For visually pleasing results,** take exact measurements of each of your walls. You'll need these measurements to calculate the dimensions of stripes and diamonds. **Whatever technique or techniques you choose, it is very important to practice** before you try a wall. If possible, work with a piece of drywall or smooth plywood 3- to 4-feet square to get a feel for a technique. **For the most successful project, keep the following painter-tested suggestions and tips in mind:**

◆ **Plan your decorative painting projects** when you have several days to work on them. Individual steps need to be done quickly, but the overall processes take time. (For small rooms, you may only need several hours a day, but you may need two or three consecutive days to accomplish the necessary steps.) ◆ **Take the time to repair your walls if necessary.** And always tape smoothly and firmly, when necessary, for your project.

◆ **Try color combinations on a practice board.** In this book, many color combinations are within the same family. Using colors that are several shades from one another on the same paint chip card gives subtle and pleasing effects. ◆ ▸ **Read paint can labels to estimate paint.** Some cans of paint cover 300 square feet of painted wall, while some specialty paints cover only half that much. For glaze, you'll generally need only half as much as you would of regular paint. ◆ **Get help if you are painting more than small wall sections.** For example, one person can successfully paint below a chair rail, above a mantel, or a small powder room. Larger areas and more difficult projects are easier when done with a partner. ◆ **Choose the sheen of your base coat** according to your project and your skill level. The higher the sheen, the more decorative coats of paint or glaze will slide around, allowing for easier manipulation. If you use a flat base coat, it will act like a sponge and absorb color from top layers of paint. ◆ **Mix commercial glaze with paint or pigment** for transparent colors for walls. When using glaze, the more glaze added to the glaze/paint mixture, the more transparent the glaze will be. Commercially available paint conditioners, when used according to directions, can add a short amount of drying time to your glazes. ◆ **Use colored pencils that match your paint colors** to mark your walls. You may not have to erase the lines, and if you do, the marks are generally easier to remove

than those of regular lead pencils. If you have to use regular lead pencils, mark or draw as lightly as possible.

◆ **Keep a supply of drop cloths and clean rags at hand.** When using rags for application or removal of paint and glaze, be consistent with the kinds of rags used. An all-cotton rag will give a different effect than a blended or synthetic fiber. Other materials, such as crumpled newspapers or plastic bags, also vary the look.

◆ **Dampen your brush with water** before painting with the latex and water-based products used in this book. This helps keep paint from quickly accumulating and drying in the bristles and makes cleanup easier. ◆ **Consider the effects of humidity on your painting.** The water-based paints used in this book dry quickly. If your house has relatively high humidity, such as on a summer day, you will have more working time than on a dry winter day. You cannot stop in the middle of a wall when you begin a step. ◆ **Step back from the wall several times during each technique** to think about the wall as a whole and get a sense of composition. ◆ **Note that the skill levels** range from the least involved to the most involved. Skill level refers to the number of steps, measuring and taping, and difficulty. The time estimates are based on 9×12-foot rooms with 8-foot ceilings, but vary depending on size, ceiling height, weather, and familiarity with the technique. For best results, read the helpful hints for techniques.

◆ **TOOLS OF THE TRADE:** Select well-made brushes designed for your particular project. Depending on the job, you'll need everything from basic paintbrushes to small artist's brushes to specialty-finish brushes. Add levels, straightedges, tapes, and combs to your supply list.

uses of color

Whatever the age and style of your home, consider the whole house when you begin to plan the color and paint finish schemes for each room.

No matter the layout of your house, you'll have occasions where you see two or more rooms at once. So it's important to consider how colors flow and decorative finishes complement each other. It's also important to remember that not every room and every surface can be the focal point. For decorative finishes to be interesting and tasteful, limit your techniques and showcased colors, and plan for plain, painted walls. These neutral spaces will make the decoratively painted walls all the more visually appealing.

This chapter will illustrate three individual paint schemes in "Whole-House Color," from homeowners that have easily and tastefully implemented interior styles of decorative painting into their homes, starting on page 32.

First, you'll be inspired by the use of basic aging techniques in a turn-of-the-century townhouse. Colors range from mellowed gold tone to a warm terra-cotta, to a greenish parchment to create interest. Upstairs, for a sitting room off the open stairwell, they chose to work with a suede finish in an olive green. The green is in a shade compatible with the aged fresco finish of an adjoining wall. Decorative painting techniques to warm and invite have enhanced each room.

Secondly, you will travel to the Far East for a contemporary Asian feel. Decorative paint finishes, chosen as part of a whole-house palette, create a

backdrop for Asian art. This personal palette, a project done by the owner and a decorative painter, illustrates how multiple paint finishes can highlight without overwhelming when colors and techniques are chosen with care.

Finally, a refurbished ranch with a hint of Spanish Colonial style for a south-of-the-border flavor. With the use of soft earthy colors, subtle yet interesting stencil motifs were used throughout the house. Architectural interest was added and revived plain, monotonous walls, without distraction to details.

This chapter also covers the use of the classic method—the "Color Wheel"—for a no-fail palette beginning on page 57, and two simple quizzes to determine your color likes and dislikes: "Discovering Your Inner Hue" on pages 58–59, and "Whose Hue to Use?" on pages 62–63.

Beginning with neutrals, for the "color-faint of heart" and how to use them, then moving on to the addition of color through decorative painting and accessories, and, finally, the use of vivid colors throughout a room, from walls to floors to decorative pieces of furniture.

In the end, your own personal style and color preference should be the main focus. So if you are timid in the hues you use, take heart, you may find your home's inner beauty in this chapter—in living color.

whole-house color

Before you choose your paint finishes and colors, assess the architectural style and detailing of your home.

updated traditional

◆ **FADED FRESCO VARIATION**, *opposite*, in the living room, emulates the look of warm, sun-washed colors of aged stucco. The technique resembles old-world garden and terrace walls. The stairwell finish replicates the faded fresco with more visible brush strokes. **See page 249 for technique.**

◆ **FADED FRESCO VARIATION**, *above*, in the living room, brightens a room with decorative woodwork and a mix of fine antiques and rich fabrics. **See page 249 for technique.**

YOU'LL BE HAPPIEST WITH THE RESULTS WHEN YOU PLAN DECORATIVE PAINTING AS A PART OF THE OVERALL INTERIOR DESIGN. Here, a restored late-19th-century townhouse offered period detailing, including trim, moldings, and a handsome mantel. The owners have a fine and ever-changing collection of antique furnishings, art, and artifacts. In this setting, they chose the faded fresco technique to give the walls of the entry and stairwell the patina of aged plaster.

Because they like the aged-plaster look for the main rooms, they chose a variation of the same technique but altered the colors from the mellow gold tones of the entry and stairwell wall to a warm terra-cotta for the formal living room. The warm tones brighten a dark entry and stairwell and play off the salvaged newel post and balusters. The shade also creates a stunning backdrop for collected antique tables, art, and interesting accessories and finds.

The terra-cotta color repeats the colors of a plaid silk chair and the decorative trim of the living room. At the same time, the flattering hue lightens a room of darker furnishings that include a leather sofa and decorative accent table. The red-based terra-cotta color of the traditionally furnished living room is balanced by the more neutral tones of the dining room color.

◆ **FADED FRESCO VARIATION**, *opposite,* in the living room, blends with the dining room's rolling and ragging finish. **See pages 248–249 for technique.**

◆ **FADED FRESCO VARIATION**, *upper left,* enriches plain walls with the depth of color and layers of texture. **See pages 248–249 for technique.**

◆ **FADED FRESCO**, *upper right,* works well with stylish faded colors. **See pages 248–249 for technique.**

◆ **ROLLING AND RAGGING**, *lower left,* a color-washed technique, creates an excellent backdrop for casually elegant interiors and furnishings. Choose lighter shades for interest. **See pages 272–273 for technique.**

◆ **ROLLING AND RAGGING**, *lower right,* lightens the look of traditional dark wood and tapestries. The finish contrasts equally well with bold and graphic contemporary art. **See pages 272–273 for technique.**

In the adjacent dining room, the parchment with green adds a subtle walled-garden effect to urn prints and urns on pedestals. A European candle chandelier above the carved table carries the decorating themes of the handsome and casually sophisticated room.

Upstairs, walls with a suede-type finish warm the sitting and television room used particularly during the cool-weather months. The deep green is also a handsome contrast to the gold-hued walls of the open, gallery-like stairwell. The green provides a stunning backdrop for additional art, a French fruitwood armoire, and a Bombay chest. For a more lighthearted vein for the remodeled bath, the owners used a technique of blending spots of paint on a white background. And for the decorative walls of the home office, they chose a muted sunset pink variation of the faded fresco finish.

◆ **FADED FRESCO**, *above left*, looks best when the colors are kept fairly light. The final color wash gives depth and character to standard drywall. **See pages 248–249 for technique.**

◆ **SUEDE**, *above right*, adds texture and the look of a beautiful sheen with a specially formulated paint that's sold under several brand names. The technique lends an air of sophistication to interiors. **See pages 280–281 for technique.**

◆ **FADED FRESCO**, *opposite*, replicates the look of time-worn plaster with a subtle technique that's an ideal backdrop. Since the technique adds the illusion of depth, faded fresco works well for walls that display art and collections, such as the grouping of a framed quilt and carved masks shown here. **See pages 248–249 for technique.**

◆ **BLENDED SPOTS**, *opposite,* add interest and depth
to a small space, such as the bathroom shown here.
The look is loosely based on marbleizing or feathering
finishes but is easier to accomplish. Neutral colors, with
only brighter colors used as accents, work best because
the technique—rather than the colors—gives the
interest. **See pages 234–235 for technique.**

◆ **BLENDED SPOTS**, *above,* are ideal for half-wall
situations, such as above the beaded-board
wainscoting, as a little goes a long way with graphic
techniques. The spots combine with the whitewashing
over the wood. **See pages 234–235 for technique.**

◆ **FADED FRESCO**, *above*, is subtle enough for areas such as this home office. Consider how techniques and paint colors contrast or blend with your trim and flooring. **See pages 248–249 for technique.**

◆ **FADED FRESCO**, *opposite*, blends easily from room to room and provides a handsome, serene backdrop for furnishings. When you base color changes on furnishings, fabrics, and art, the differences between rooms can be noticeable enough to be interesting. **See pages 248–249 for technique.**

far east **suburban**

When you move or decide to redecorate, seize the opportunity to create a home that reflects your interests and color preferences.

IF YOUR WALLS ARE PLAIN WHITE AND YOUR FLOORING NEUTRAL, CONSIDER THEM A CLEAN SLATE FOR A NEW BEGINNING. Start with the positives of what you love and open your imagination to the possibilities of an innovative color palette and decorative paint finishes. As a first step, think about how much light your rooms receive and the effects of flooring and woodwork on color choices. Concentrate your decorative finishes as accent walls for larger, open rooms—particularly those with vaulted or unusually high ceilings. Save overall specialty finishes for rooms of standard size and ceiling height, and more intricate finishes for smaller focal points. When you are decorating several rooms at one time, choose a finish appropriate to the mood and use of each room.

This suburban townhouse is an illustrative case in point with its vaulted ceiling and open space. The owner successfully used a variety of paint finishes to define the moods of rooms used for different purposes. The project began with the owner's collection of Asian art and his interest in the Far East. New upholstered pieces, chosen to work with the art, set the color scheme for the vaulted living room that opens to the stairwell and

the dine-in kitchen. The colors also carry over to the home office and the powder room.

Because of the sheer amount of wall space, the owner first planned the background walls that would not be decoratively finished. He chose a warm, neutral tan that would work throughout and wisely started with the living room, the largest and most visible room of the two-story

◆ **DOUBLE-ROLLED**, *opposite,* creates a focal point for architecture, art, and collections. In this townhouse, the two rolled colors transform a standard mantel into a gallery-like setting for the owner's Asian art. **See pages 246–247 for technique.**

◆ **DOUBLE-ROLLED**, *right,* repeats the tones of the art, such as the masks, but with enough variations for contrast and texture. **See pages 246–247 for technique.**

townhouse. Instead of a piecemeal approach, he planned the palette for the whole house so the colors and finishes play off each other and highlight his art. In the living room, the natural focal point of the fireplace takes on more importance with a rolled finish that emulates the textured colors of dried leaves. This backdrop frames a mantel arrangement of carved masks and pottery.

The adjacent kitchen, visible from the entry and living room, features two shades of green to blend with favorite Japanese prints. The wall below the chair rail is combed in a creamy linen color over the deeper green. Such accent walls are ideal for combing, a handsome but fairly painstaking technique.

To give the other main downstairs room the character of a library retreat, the owner decided on a leather-type technique in shades of aged gold. Handsome in its own right, the finish brightens a room that receives little daylight and complements the oak woodwork. The adjacent red powder room highlights carved masks.

◆ **SOLID TAN**, *above left*, provides the crucial neutral space in a townhouse with six decorative paint finishes. Decorative finishes can be overpowering in areas with vaulted ceilings and large expanses of wall space. Instead, take advantage of the luxury of open space for a gallery display.

◆ **SOLID TAN**, *above right*, blends with the colors of fabrics and accessories as well as decorative finishes.

◆ **SOLID GREEN AND COMBING**, *opposite*, play off each other to add visual design interest to the townhouse's informal dining area. Combing is easy to do with the proper tools and is effective in small spaces. Here, combing creates the look of wainscoting below the chair rail. The framed Japanese prints inspired the moss green color choice. **See pages 244–245 for combing technique.**

Upstairs, two favorite shades of blue and two finishes set the schemes for the master bedroom and meditation room. Bedroom walls are painted with commercially available, suede-finish paint. The meditation room, planned to emulate the serenity of a Far East garden, appears as though walls are covered with sheer chambray cloth. Instead, they are painted with a combination of horizontal and vertical dragging.

And in the pièce de résistance, the upstairs bath features all the colors in the palette, except red, painted as a sporty, tailored plaid.

◆ **LEATHER**, *opposite,* ages new spaces, such as this townhouse's home office. The technique is ideal for rooms with a library look and feel. Here, a golden leather tone energizes a room with dark oak furniture and little natural light. **See pages 262–263. for technique.**

◆ **SOLID RED**, *above,* illustrates the appeal of an interesting color for rooms that serve as balances to decorative finishes. If you are unused to strong color, consider one for a small area such as this stylish bath.

◆ **PLAID**, *left,* recalls the popular woven fabric. The technique is based on simple sponging but requires careful measuring. Choose the technique for rooms, such as this windowless bath, where a small area can yield large decorative impact. Here, the plaid uses most of the colors in the townhouse's color palette. **See pages 266–267 for technique.**

◆ **CHAMBRAY**, *opposite,* recalls the woven texture of the classic work shirt fabric. The technique is related to linen as it is created with specialty brushes, which are sold in kits. Here, in a cool blue color, the technique reflects the calm of a meditation room with Far Eastern influences. The technique would translate well into a charming bedroom when paired with white furnishings. **See pages 236–237 for technique.**

◆ **CHAMBRAY**, *top,* relaxes a small, private room used for meditation. Soft colors work best for this low-key finish. **See pages 236–237 for technique.**

◆ **SUEDE**, *bottom,* adds texture, through a specially formulated paint, to plain walls. Here, the owner chose blue for a peaceful bedroom that adjoins his meditation room. The two blues blend without competing. **See pages 280–281 for technique.**

spanish colonial style

A chair-rail border, created from glaze and subtle stencil motifs, dresses up the open living spaces of a remodeled California ranch.

CONSIDER STENCILED CHAIR RAILS OR OTHER SIMILARLY SUBDUED TECHNIQUES TO IMPART ARCHITECTURAL INTEREST TO PLAIN LIVING OR DINING AREAS. As a first step, choose a design motif compatible with both the style of your home and your decorating taste. Look at existing features, such as a decorative fireplace surround or the pattern in a fabric or rug, for inspiration. For an interesting backdrop that does not overpower, choose a simplified design that blends with your wall color. Study the placement of windows, doors, and other openings to determine the most pleasing height. For an easier alternative, stencil the chair rail directly below your windows.

◆ A major remodeling transformed a standard ranch-style home with hints of gracious Spanish Colonial style. The stenciled chair-rail border, *right,* adds interesting detailing to the open living room and calls attention to the arched doorway and narrow casement windows. The arch frames a view into the dining room, detailed with the same mosaic-style stencil. Neutral colors animate the open spaces without competing with the handsomely detailed sconces and sophisticated furnishings.

◆ *right:* In a subtle technique, the wall area used as a chair rail is glazed and stenciled. The border aligns with muntins of the French windows for a neat appearance. Warm shades of tan balance the plank floor and provide a soothing background for a collection of antique and reproduction furniture, including the gently curved desk and European-style armchair. Accessories, such as the antique lantern and old books, enhance the sophisticated, yet muted, wall detailing.

◆ *left:* Gentle arches frame the views from room to room in the open plan. The sophisticated glazed and stenciled chair rail enlivens the living room and adjoining dining room without distracting from the arches and narrow French windows—both key elements of the Spanish Colonial style. Sofas face each other in the center of the room, allowing the chair rail to be the backdrop for a cupboard display and a pair of flanking chairs. Walls showcase collected contemporary art.

◆ *opposite:* Soft, earthy colors and a raised tiled hearth impart a sense of the patio garden to the recessed fireplace. The stenciled chair rail wraps the opening of the arch, cleverly detailing the space. The burnt bamboo plant stand gives a strong silhouette against the stenciling, while the patterned rug adds a complementary pattern for design interest. The curved detailing of the iron sconce recalls the stencil's exotic curves.

◆ *opposite:* The stenciled ceiling medallion repeats and balances the motifs of the chair-rail border in the formal dining room. To enrich the Spanish Colonial flavor, bullnose edges replace window casings. The bamboo shade controls light and views without the intrusion of fussy treatments. The monochromatic color scheme replicates the sophisticated palette seen throughout the house. Scrollwork—from the stenciled border to the cast table base to the carved detailing of the chairs—unifies the room. Overscaled pieces, such as the scrolled table base and sideboard, give substance to the setting.

The leaning mirror, with egg-and-dart molding, imparts a sophisticated backdrop to the print and obelisk.

◆ *left:* The stenciled and glazed medallion recalls the traditional, ornate plaster medallions of grand 18th- and 19th-century homes. The shape repeats the curves of the reproduction metal and glass-globe chandelier. The placement of the motifs to decorative points and the mosaic effects allude to the exotic Moorish influences that appear in 1920s interpretations of Spanish-style houses. Frosted globes direct light to the ceiling medallion.

PRIMARY   SECONDARY

TERTIARY   MONOCHROMATIC

WHY USE THE COLOR WHEEL? This classic method helps you create a no-fail color palette. When you are beginning to decorate with color or when you are changing your palette, start with your favorite color and work with schemes based on the groupings of primary, secondary, tertiary, and monochromatic. Choose only one color as your focus and allow colors in your chosen group to be accents. (See the color wheel here.) When you stay within one classic grouping, you aren't clashing colors even in the brightest primaries. Or, even easier, choose a favorite and add close and easy-to-relate color wheel neighbors as congenial accents. Use white for relief and black for sophisticated accents.

the color **wheel**

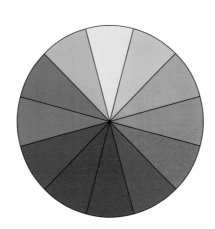

PRIMARY: Color your decorating with the classic crayon primaries of red, yellow, and blue. When used in the same intensities and in varying amounts, the three are a natural for cheerful, family-friendly rooms. For the power of a single primary color, choose your favorite of the three and balance it with wood tones and neutral accents.

SECONDARY: Green is from blue and yellow, orange from yellow and red, and purple from red and blue. You'll likely look beyond the clearest secondary colors to tints and shades. Green is enjoying a revival. The look can be light or lively depending on the shades and accents you choose. Often tricky, sponged shades of orangey terra-cotta brighten dark green walls.

TERTIARY: Depending on your perspective, color gets fun or a little tricky at this third stage. Now we are into the equal mixes of primary plus its closest secondary color—blue-green, yellow-green, red-orange, red-purple, and blue-purple. Or, try the look without major color commitment by adding tertiary touches, such as the blue-purple pillows, to a neutral scheme.

MONOCHROMATIC: Remember one-color decorating isn't one-shade or one-tint decorating. It also isn't restricted to neutrals. Instead you are using one color that appeals to you and introducing variations in texture and materials and in shades and tints.

discovering your inner hue

THE COLORS OF YOUR EVERYDAY LIFE HAVE A PROFOUND EFFECT ON YOUR MOODS AND EMOTIONS EVEN WHEN YOU'RE NOT AWARE OF THEM. You associate just about everything you do, the places you occupy, what you wear, and what you own with particular colors. And each of these brings with it feelings, moods, and memories—excited or calm, energizing or restful, pleasant or unpleasant.

Do you want to open your eyes to your true color feelings—and put the emotional power of color association to work for you? Complete the following fun and informative inventory of activities and related colors. Use a separate sheet of paper and compare the results with a friend. Then calculate your color preferences and use the results to help you decorate your home into the happiest environment possible. When you know your own personal color associations, you can surround yourself with the shades that reflect your moods throughout the day and that enhance the purpose of every room in your home.

COLOR AND ACTIVITY INVENTORY

For insight on your color preferences, think about the color you associate with the listed activities: Ask yourself what color you would like to wear or be surrounded by as you do it.

Choice	Color
1. Going to bed	_____
2. Eating breakfast	_____
3. Lounging in your bathrobe	_____
4. Soaking in the tub	_____
5. Applying make-up	_____
6. Polishing your nails	_____
7. Driving in your car	_____
8. Picking field flowers	_____
9. Harvesting your garden	_____
10. Coloring your hair	_____
11. Tying a scarf or tie	_____
12. Setting the table	_____
13. Going to a fancy ball	_____
14. Eating at your favorite restaurant	_____
15. Lighting a candelabra for a romantic dinner	_____
16. Putting up the patio umbrella	_____
17. Placing a wreath on the front door	_____
18. Sitting with a refreshing drink	_____
19. Reading in front of the fire	_____
20. Mowing the lawn	_____
21. Dressing for work	_____
22. Biking with friends	_____
23. Swimming in the ocean	_____
24. Jogging after work	_____
25. Kayaking down a river	_____
26. Daydreaming at home	_____
27. Cooking for the holidays	_____
28. Talking on the telephone with your best friend	_____
29. Dining with good friends	_____
30. Celebrating getting the job	_____
31. Holding a wine tasting	_____
32. Attending a country wedding	_____
33. Arranging a bowl of fruit	_____
34. Critiquing a favorite painting	_____

SCORING

Now designate each of your color choices according to three basic categories of color association—warm, cool, and neutral colors. First, find your colors in the following category lists:

Warm Colors: Red, Orange, Yellow, Pink
Cool Colors: Blue, Green, Purple
Neutral Colors: Black, Brown, White, Gray, Beige, Taupe

Next, assign an "A" wherever you have listed a warm color, a "B" for all your cool color choices, and a "C" for neutral colors. Count how many you listed in each category.

Use the information below to see what your choices may say about you and where you can use colors to your advantage in every room of your home.

Your Tally: Warm____   Cool____   Neutral____

SCORING KEY FOR COLOR CATEGORIES

Warm Colors: Active colors that move forward, communicate vigor, cheer you up, excite passions, inspire conversation, and force emotions.

Cool Colors: Passive colors that recede into the background, cool you down, calm your nerves, lift your spirits, promote meditation, and generally comfort the soul.

Neutral Colors: Open-minded colors that are easy on the eye, symbolize a down-to-earth attitude, make you feel safe and secure, and lend a cooperative air.

HOW DO YOU COMPARE?

• *Mostly "A"s?* You come alive with energizing colors. Use these in the active rooms of your home: entryways, hallways, dining rooms, rooms for entertaining, and playrooms. Also, enliven neutral rooms with a warm accent color.

• *Mostly "B"s?* You respond to soothing colors. Use them in rooms for rest and relaxation such as the bedroom, living room, home office, spa, or sunporch.

• *Mostly "C"s?* You like to play it safe. Neutral colors are perfect for rooms that connect to other rooms, or rooms where you spend a great deal of time, such as kitchens and bathrooms.

• *Tie with two or all categories?* Evenly distribute your color "temperatures" throughout your home in doses that are compatible to the room's purpose. Bridge warm and cool colors with neutrals.

create **comfort**

IF YOU AREN'T SURE HOW MUCH COLOR YOU WANT IN YOUR LIFE, THINK ABOUT HOW YOU USE COLOR. If you collect pottery or porcelains or if you just enjoy a particular color, you have the tools to introduce and blend inspiring touches of colors throughout your home. Here , the subtle greens and yellows of Depression-era pottery inspired the living and dining room color schemes. Walls and trim remain safely white. Choose two complementary colors for interesting, versatile accents when the backdrop remains white or a subtle neutral.

◆ *right:* Start at your own comfort level. Here, the muted yellow tones soften the scheme with the window treatment and gathered chandelier cord. Accessories, such as a mirror and candleholders, contrast with texture and form.

whose hue to use?

BORED WITH BEIGE? Feeling ennui with off-white walls? Don't be afraid to bring the power and personality of color into your home. Following a few simple guidelines, you can change the way you feel when you walk into a room and even how big that room looks. And, if you are confused by the rainbow of color choices, the following questions and answers will help you understand the power of color—and help put it to work for you.

Q Can color change your mood from "blah" to "bouncy"? Color creates a zone of feeling much like a "psychological thermostat." Red, orange, and yellow are sunny, energizing, even "hot" colors. They bring warmth and life to a room, stimulating conversation, appetites, and passion. On the other hand, blues, greens, and purples are cooling colors. They turn down the "heat," creating a calming and restful atmosphere.

Q How do you set the "color temperature" throughout your home? First, think of how the room will be used. Choose warm colors for lively and active areas, such as the kitchen or dining room. Cool colors are best suited for areas of rest and relaxation—the living room and bedrooms.

Consider the natural light and location of rooms as well. For a chilly room, or one with north-facing windows, use warm colors to bring a welcome coziness. Similarly, a south-facing room with blazing sunlight will benefit from cool colors that create a temperate climate.

Warm reds, oranges, and yellows draw walls in, making a large room seem cozier and more intimate. But cool blues, greens, and purples will make it appear larger. Use this power of color on walls and ceilings to change the space of your room without expensive construction.

Q What colors are comfortable—and comforting—for you? Color preference is intensely personal, often based on associations from your past and stimulated by everyday experiences. Choose colors that you associate with pleasant times and places. Think of colors that remind you of your favorite things: red rubies, green apples, sunny blue skies, purple sunsets.

Check out your clothing closet: it will give you a clear palette of the colors that make you happy every day. Stay away from the latest fads in colors—let your personal style shine through.

If you like to keep things light, pastel colors may be your best selections. They contain a lot of white, which reflects light, creating airy spaces. Use a cool pastel blue to make a room "grow" and appear restful, spacious, and calm.

Q **Do you want to keep things dark, deep, and dramatic?** Dark colors absorb light, creating intimate, cozy spaces. Use deep red, tobacco brown, coal black, and hunter green for dramatic passages, such as entryways, hallways, and stairways. Dark colors are also perfect choices for small rooms where you want to heighten the intimate atmosphere and for large rooms that have a lot of sunlight, windows, and doors.

Q **Can you use "plain shades" as mood makers?** Yes. Natural shades, such as gray, beige, taupe, and ivory, are actually neutral "uncolors" that rely on clever use of light and texture to create shadows for very atmospheric rooms. For interest, vary textures and materials, from smooth metals and warm woods to rough linens or burlaps.

Whites and ivories reflect light and bounce it off walls and surfaces to make a space feel bright and airy. Like green, these colors remind us of items found in nature, connecting us with the great outdoors.

Q **Can color give you a sensual "feeling" or change your environment?** Colors often evoke the sensory, tactile "feel" of different items. Shades of wheat, moss green, and mustard yellow recall earthy textures and natural objects and substances. "Jewel" colors—deep purple, deep red, and gold—give the feeling of luxurious fabric textures and riches.

To quickly change the mood, choose neutral colors for your walls and upholstery and swap the colors of your pillows, area rugs, and lampshades to coordinate with the seasons: Use lively pinks and blues for summer; terra-cottas and gold for autumn; reds, blacks, and whites for winter; and shades of green for the coming of spring.

Q **Why choose paint to give your room a perfect "complexion"?** Wall paint is easy to use, quick, and usually the least expensive way to give a room an instant "makeover." Like cosmetics, it can mask less-than-perfect details and call attention to fine ones. Flat paint finishes are subdued compared to semigloss or gloss paints, which intensify colors.

Q **Can you use window dressings to jazz up your room color?** Window dressings are powerful color elements in a room, as the eye is drawn to the light of a window. Double the impact of your window dressings by lining them with a colored or patterned cloth and tying them back to expose the underside.

The type of lining is also important. If the lining is lightweight and light colored, drapery colors will intensify and glow as sunlight passes through them. A "black out" lining that is denser and heavier will literally block light and subdue (or deaden) the drapery colors.

Q **Can you get color impact from what's underfoot?** A floor carpeted in light solid color—the same as the wall color—will make a room grow. For the opposite effect, use area rugs (especially dark colors) to shrink the room by visually breaking up the floor space. Also, a highly polished wood floor reflects light.

Q **Do you notice what happens when you turn on the light?** Choose the right bulb for your room color. Incandescent bulbs will "warm" your room colors with a yellowish tone. Incandescent light can make pale yellows practically disappear, some greens turn yellow-green, and clay colors turn orange. Fluorescent lighting casts a bluish color—making reds turn deep raspberry and yellows turn a greenish hue. (Color-corrected bulbs, without these effects, are available but expensive.)

Q **What colors can you use to give your home a vintage appearance?** Use "tea" colors that simulate aged materials. (These are colors that appear to be aged; they have the patina of old fabrics and wallpaper.) You can even give new natural cotton or linen fabrics this look by dipping them in a bath of a tea-and-water solution.

Q **How can you plan a whole-house scheme? Should colors match exactly?** A total-home scheme is just a larger version of a single room's color scheme. Consider the position of the rooms and their flow from one room to another. For easy transition, start with a color or two you like and vary the colors, accents, and intensities as you move from room to room. For a small home or a home with an open plan, paint the public rooms in one light color or tints of one color.

Often the most charming and successful interiors are those that offer colors in unusual combinations and off "matches." Perfectly matched colors can be dull and look too contrived.

Q **Can a bit of paint or accessories change a room when there's no time to do the walls?** For a big impact, paint the ceiling a color other than white. Or paint the fireplace a different color than your moldings; use a paint technique on a wood floor; paint the back wall of bookshelves or cupboards a different color than the front.

Inexpensive accessories can be the "jewelry" of a well-dressed room. Change your plain lampshades to colored ones or add a colorful fringe to the bottom of a plain shade. Display colorful collections of balls of yarn, glassware, or shells to give added spark without spending a lot of money.

working with white

WHEN YOUR GOAL IS LIGHT AND AIRY, START WITH WHITE. White walls and trim work—anywhere in your home. Because your walls aren't competing, you're free to introduce colors through your choices of fabrics, art, and accessories. Keep in mind the many, many variations of white, from the cool and stark to the warm and soft. Just as you would with color, experiment with several shades of white to find the right one for your room. If you are using white in a sun-filled room, remember to look at your color samples at different times of the day and at night with artificial light. In all-white rooms, such as these sunporches, vary the whites from cool to warm for interest. As white can appear cold, use textures and accents, such as homey quilts, pottery, baskets, and plants for inviting warmth.

◆ *opposite:* Make the most of the freedom of white walls and furnishings to introduce a mix of pretty florals and patchwork fabrics. For a relaxed look, rather than a jarring contrast, choose patterned fabrics that include whites and pastels. If you prefer a tailored look, you can't go wrong with a sporty red, white, and blue scheme.

◆ *above:* When your idea of a library leans to porch decor rather than dark paneling, paint the built-ins white and add white furniture, such as these always-classic wicker pieces. Use fabrics, such as the quilt, for a cozy, curl-up-and-read ambience.

◆ *right:* Plant-filled sunrooms and sunporches are traditionally white and with good reason. Color would be a distraction where windows frame views and blur the distinction between indoors and out.

COLOROPTIONS *It's always summer when you pair pretty pastels with white. Add touches of gray to give a white and pastel room a more sophisticated edge.*

PART OF THE FUN OF DECORATING IS IN EXPERIMENTING. When you start with a neutral backdrop and noncolors of wood and iron, even tiny touches stand out. If you are beginning a room or updating colors, begin with small easy-to-change touches. Here, the yellow and green accents could be phase one of enriching a room with color. When you are comfortable with your first forays, add more accents from your chosen color or branch out into other hues that blend or contrast.

color without commitment

◆ *opposite:* When color comes from a collection of objects, such as the pottery in this corner cupboard, group the pieces for impact. The effect is strong and avoids the haphazard look of small objects placed around a room. Repeat your accent colors, too, for unity. Here, the glasses on the table and the simple window treatment unify the scheme without disturbing the harmony. Accent pillows and throws are quick-to-add and easy-to-change elements that reinforce color choices.

◆ *above:* When you play two accent colors—here yellow and green—against a neutral scheme, choose one as your primary player. To warm the room above, yellow does double duty as the window treatment and the glassware. Touches of red would further enliven and warm the scheme for cozy fireside entertaining. Or simply switching to a green window treatment and glasses would create a cooler, more summery look. With subtle backdrops, small color changes count.

color quick!

WHEN YOU ARE READY FOR INSTANT AND READILY-AVAILABLE COLOR, ACCENT WITH JUST ONE OR TWO BRIGHT ACCESSORIES. Catalogues and home stores are chock-full of bright, moderately-priced pillows in patterns and solids. And, flea markets and craft shows yield colorful, affordable pieces. Even one or two touches have major impact against a noncolor scheme. Easiest of all, peruse your neighborhood grocery store, the farmer's market, and the flower shop for temporary touches. Save the colorful blue or green empties from bottled water. Vary sizes and shapes for interest. Or, brighten your rooms with blooming plants and fresh flowers. One bright flower, in mass, creates more color impact than a mixed bouquet.

◆ *right:* Think of a white kitchen and neutral upholstery as a canvas for your creativity. For the most impact, introduce the dynamics of primary colors. Here, red, yellow, and blue all play a part in energizing the scheme. Remember to repeat the colors so your palette looks planned, instead of random. For color without clutter, rotate and change accessories rather than adding to the mix. *Alternative:* Try prints and patterns in warmer yellow or softer green tones instead of blue and red.

COLOROPTIONS Give the primaries a twist by going beyond crayon box colors to orangey reds or lemony yellows paired with cobalt blue or vivid green. The trick for a harmonious look is to keep colors in the same intensity (degree of brightness). An easy way is to choose colors in the same place on the color chips.

◆ *above:* Neutral and sophisticated, the comfortable living room mixes tailored cotton duck sofas with country-style pieces and folk art. Fill a favorite pottery piece with the brightest flowers you can find to make it come alive. In the early spring, try branches from flowering trees or in the fall, autumn foliage. When flowers are scarce, bowls of fruit are alternatives.

◆ *right:* Color comes as easily as a grouping of pottery, vases, and plates. As you look for pieces, work with one strong hue, here the blue, to anchor and unify your scheme.

EVEN IF YOU PREFER WHITE WALLS, YOU CAN LIVE WITH MORE COLOR THAN YOU THINK. For a quick start, group your most colorful accessories, such as pottery, quilts, art, and pillows. Just the addition of a flea market piece or two may be enough to fill out your more colorful scheme. If you like the idea of vibrant wall color, test the waters by painting one accent wall in your color choice. Later, if the shade feels right to you, you can finish the job or even paint the other walls in another, complementary, color.

neutral beginnings

◆ *opposite:* Repeat colors for a feeling of pleasing unity. Rather than a hodge-podge collection of disparate objects, this room feels carefully planned. The repeated shades of blue and green from the paintings set the tone for the pottery and charmingly distressed, odd-size shutters.

◆ *left:* Paint a wall or part of a wall in a bold (or more discreet) color and see how you live with the color. For a pulled-together look, repeat your focal-point color in smaller doses, such as pillows and candles.

◆ *below:* One jolt of color wakes up a neutral room. Here, flowers in the still life painting and red in the quilts inspired the oversized pillow.

COLOROPTIONS *Small touches of an interesting color wake up a room. Consider purples, teals, and deep pinks as alternatives to red or blue.*

COLOROPTIONS

Pink and Azure Blue

Lemon Yellow and Mint Green

Aquamarine and Seafoam

Hyacinth and Lilac

Lime Green and Cobalt

Apricot and Peach

Tangerine and Melon

light & bright

ENJOY A SUMMER MOOD ALL YEAR WITH A PALETTE INSPIRED BY LIGHTHEARTED PALES OR HAPPY VIBRANT HUES. To cool a climate with a long, hot summer, try a scheme based on the palest of pastels, as this bedroom at the beach illustrates. Generous touches of white keep the setting crisp, not sweet. Or, if brights are your style, experiment with some of the newest combinations that rev up shades of blues and greens or unexpected palettes into dynamic decorating. The fun of color is how easily you create a new look and set a personal mood with fresh backgrounds or just quick accents.

◆ *opposite:* In a serene setting, use the merest hint of a pale tint for your wall color. Lighten a pretty pastel with white for a kiss of color. Here, the tint is seashell pink. For an unexpected twist, add a vibrant note such as the painted library ladder.

IN TODAY'S NO-BOUNDARIES SCHEMES, THINK OF WHITE AS HALF OF A COLORFUL DECORATING DUO. If you enjoy an intense color, such as sunshine yellow, stripe your walls. The effect will be colorful but still airy. With clean white as the background, every accessory, from artwork to the tiniest teacup, stands out. Pastels are pretty, as soft shades are amplified by white.

punch up white

◆ *opposite:* Think of a pale interior as a neutral backdrop that's easy to change with accessories and art. Though the walls and upholstered pieces are light, the distinctive oil painting hung by a decorative rope sets a nautical theme. A watercolor, pottery, and floral fabrics could transform the room into cottage style. Sleek accessories could impart a contemporary spirit.

◆ *above:* Use a pale scheme as the ideal backdrop to mix furnishings and accessories. When you keep the walls, floors, and major pieces light, accessories, tableware, and linens take center stage. Distressed or color-washed pieces, such as this armoire used for storage, are ideal for touches of color that don't overpower the palette. Traditional country-style cool blues and greens, in distressed finishes, work in pale rooms.

COLOROPTIONS *Yellow not you? Try greens, pinks, or periwinkle blue to stripe with white. Look for such alternative choices for every color scheme featured throughout this chapter.*

COLOR**OPTIONS**

hints of gold

ENRICH EVER-VERSATILE, EVER-STYLISH WHITE WITH THE POWER OF METALLIC GOLD. As gold is such a powerful attention-getter, just a few touches are sufficient to play against white walls, a light floor, and pristine white upholstery. For easy touches, consider an oversized framed mirror and a gilded chair or table. Or, as gold accessories are readily available, add such touches as a throw, small silk accent pillows, candlesticks, porcelains, pottery pieces, a lamp base, or picture frames. The trick is restraint: Use no other colors in the room—white for the walls and major furniture pieces—with art and accents used sparingly. Or, if you like a rich, warmer alternative, paint your walls in one of the handsome muted gold shades and pair with white accessories.

COLOR**OPTIONS**

◆ *left:* For instant chic style, marry gold and white. Resist the temptation for all-gold accessories. Here, crystal vases are a lighter look for varying heights of fresh lilies and assorted greenery.

◆ *right:* A painted floorcloth finishes a white-and-gold scheme in style and adds subtle pattern to the sleek room. As an alternative, consider a pale finish for a wood floor or off-white or palest gold carpet. Distressed gold finishes, such as this French-style armchair, give texture, rather than shine.

COLOR*OPTIONS*

Beyond the glitter of gold, pair white with metallic shades of silver or pewter. Or try accents of cooler pinks for unexpected hints of color.

◆ *above:* Look to the traditional style of Early American houses for interesting ways to introduce color. Here, the chair rail and window trim imbue the dining room with color. The walls are a supporting tint. For interest and in keeping with the period style, the baseboard is painted slate black. To tie the spare look and subtle scheme together, the hanging corner cupboard repeats the green of the painted table.

◆ *opposite:* One brightly painted piece of furniture can be all you need to jazz up a plain white room. Here, an old bed was simply painted with a fire engine shade of red enamel for a vibrant jolt of color. Use accents—the quilt and pillows—to tie such a contrasting scheme together and avoid a choppy look. **COLOROPTIONS** *To make your touches count, choose a bold color—warm gold and pumpkin or cooler purple and teal.*

touches of color

WHEN YOU ARE GETTING COMFORTABLE WITH MORE COLOR IN YOUR HOME, THINK HOW TO CREATIVELY INTRODUCE EASY-TO-LIVE-WITH TOUCHES AND ACCENTS. If you have been living with white or off-white walls and want to see how more color feels to you, reverse the standard of colorful walls and white trim. Instead, paint the chair rail or other woodwork in your color choice and use a pale, subtle tint of the same color for the walls. An easy method is to use the deepest, most intense shade on a paint chip for the trim and the palest tint on the same chip for the wall color. To get the most impact from your trim color, choose a semigloss paint for light-reflecting shine.

COLOR**OPTIONS**

relax with **blue** & green

HOW YOU PAIR COLORS MEANS AS MUCH TO YOUR ROOM SCHEME AS THE COLORS YOU CHOOSE. Blue and green are neighbors on the cool side of the color wheel—with restful shades of blue-green flowing between pure green and pure blue. It's easiest to pair different colors of the same intensity—such as bright blue and bright green. But, as the colors are closely related, a dramatic look combines a pale or yellow-green with a darker, vibrant cobalt blue. To keep the mood fresh and fun, use the lighter green for larger surfaces, such as walls. As cobalt blue is a dominating color, restrict it to accent furniture pieces or accessories and add white for relief.

◆ *above left:* Enjoy these stylish colors with a painted checkerboard wall treatment of 4×4-inch squares. Experiment with combinations of blue and green by painting squares on cardboard or wallboard until you find the shades that you like.

◆ *above right*: Consider soft, pale shades of green neutrals that pair well with yellows and pinks as well as blues.

◆ *opposite:* Use a shade of yellow-green for a warm approach to a cool color. For fun, look for a fabric that has the yellow-green you like. Choose blending but not matching paint chips for other greens. Before you paint walls or furniture, tape up color chips you like as sunlight will dramatically alter shades of yellow-green. Cobalt, rather than darker navy or midnight blue, contrasts without overpowering the greens.

COLOROPTIONS *For other blue-green pairs or accents, if you prefer, use two shades of blue or two of green for a monochromatic scheme.*

moods of blue

FROM THE SLEEKEST CONTEMPORARY TO THE COZIEST COLONIAL, BLUE WORKS IN YOUR DECORATING SCHEME. Cool and restful, blue is associated visually and aesthetically with peace and serenity. Think of the sea and the outdoors and the expanse of the sky. Light tints of blue open up a room, keeping the feel airy and summer fresh. (Tint the ceiling paint, too, for just a hint of coolness.) Dark, intense blues, such as cobalt or royal, give a room weight and drama. Beyond the walls, window treatments in rich brocades and velvets have traditionally been blue, trimmed with gold. Or, follow the example of nature and mix blues for a room that sings a gentle song. Use pale blue for your walls and darker, grayed blue for trim. Or, mix grayed blues with clear medium and dark navy blues. When you are not sure of what blue to use, pick out a paint chip and try swatches of the lightest and darkest shades. To quickly warm a blue scheme, introduce green, yellow, or red accents.

◆ *opposite:* With easy style, shades of blue create a restful, simple bedroom. Go beyond walls to doors and ceiling to surround yourself with the blues of sea, sky, and summer flowers.

◆ *above left:* Employ blue to emphasize, but not overshadow, architecture in a contemporary setting. Here, the blue niche effectively "frames" a white-matted print.

◆ *above right:* Classic Colonial blue, often seen in 18th-century-style interiors, gives the appropriate backdrop for a collection of pewter pieces. Seasonal yellow daffodils seem to pop to life against the darker background.

COLOROPTIONS There's a blue for any taste. Intense cobalt blues to pale tropical shades to fun turquoises.

red,white & blue

THE COLORS OF OLD GLORY, THIS TRICOLOR COMBINATION HAS LONG BEEN ASSOCIATED WITH FLAGS AND FESTIVITIES, SAILING SHIPS AND CELEBRATIONS. Crisp and breezy, red, white, and blue naturally decorate porches and playrooms, kids' rooms and nurseries. Try it, too, with stripes and plaids for an All-American living room or slipcover upholstered pieces in summer whites or striped seersuckers for a nautical, seaside feel. For the most versatility, choose a soft white for the background—or ever-so-subtle blue-and-white pinstripes. Fabric choices are wide-ranging, from the classic casuals of sturdy denims, chambrays, and corduroys to more formal dark red or blue cotton damasks or dyed linens. Or, for cozy warmth, consider red, white, and blue overscaled checks or plaids with red accents.

COLOROPTIONS For your tricolor scheme, match the red to the intensity of blue and/or yellow.

◆ *top left:* The three-color-plus-yellow scheme creates the perfect foil for a living room or family room

based on All-American style. The striped sofa, crisp seersucker for sticky summer weather, warms up in winter with a solid blue denim or red-white-and-blue plaid flannel slipcover.

◆ *above:* Sleek with traditional overtones, this quilt-inspired bedroom exemplifies the versatility of cool blue and white with touches of bright red accents. Though the look is decidedly tailored red, white, and blue, it could take on a different decorating personality with toile or floral pillows replacing the quilts. Or, with a patterned or plaid duvet, lush throws for bed and easy chair, and extra pillows, the room could be filled with curl-up-and-read warmth.

blue & white & yellow

Classic for spring gardens and for decorating, blue and yellow pair two popular primaries into one of the prettiest, freshest combinations. Almost opposites on the color wheel (see page 57), they create the excitement of opposite attraction. Deep blues and vibrant yellows set a dramatic tone in a living or formal dining room. Or, in paler tints, blues and yellows are perfect for kitchens, family rooms, bedrooms, nurseries, or porches. Again, depending on your furnishings and accessories, the look can easily range from European to American Country to contemporary. To warm up this scheme, paint the walls a soft sunshine, butter, or mustard yellow. Or, for a cooler, more restful look, perfect for a bedroom, choose a pale blue for your walls and accent with white.

◆ *above:* Blue and white warm against sunshine-yellow walls. When gently distressed pieces are the focal points, choose a delicate shade that won't compete with your antiquing finds.

◆ *top:* Love blue and yellow? Want a sophisticated and versatile look? Play dark blue and bright yellow fabrics, covering classic furnishings, against a neutral sofa and creamy walls and window treatments. Choose a dark rug to anchor the scheme and balance the airy backdrop. Add blue accent accessories. With this refreshed look, your favorites sing a jazzy new tune.

◆ *bottom opposite:* Collectors of blue-and-white porcelains and pottery, especially the blue willow pattern, are a legion. These favorites shine against a background of lemon or butter-yellow. Painted the same lemon-yellow as the dining room, the entry and stairwell extend the happy color. Lovers of blue and yellow often expand their collecting, mixing yellow and blue-and-yellow pieces with their blue and white. The more the merrier works here. **COLOROPTIONS** *From palest straw to rich wheat gold, shades of yellow are the happiest partners for beloved blues.*

sunshine yellows

◆ *above left:* For color without claustrophobia, paint a small, windowless powder room in a buttery shade. The background creates a soft glow for sconces and pretty floral fabrics often used in such dressy settings. If your walls are in good condition, choose paint with a semigloss finish for the pleasant effect of shine and for light reflection.

◆ *above right:* Though pale and airy, the lightest tints of yellow warm a traditional-style dining room without intense color. With just a hint of pale color, this yellow allows the antique chairs and painted pedestal table to be the focal points. Note the subtle contrast between the white table and the pale sunlight of the walls. A more vibrant shade would create a jarring contrast not as visually pleasing and not as easy to live with. Such a subtle yellow tint provides a soft backdrop for delicate prints, art, and plates as well as silver and china.

COLOROPTIONS

A CLASSIC, YELLOW HAS GOOD CHEER THAT ENLIVENS FORMAL LIVING AND DINING ROOMS AS EFFEC-
TIVELY. No room, from the most casual to the most formal, is immune to the power of this happiest
color. Reputed to lift spirits, yellow gives the glow of the sun to dark, cheerless spaces and stands up
to the color-draining powers of a wall of windows on a western exposure. With the ever-increasing
paint choices, you'll easily find the palest tints perfect for porches, nurseries, and sunrooms to clear
yellows to shades of mustard popular for country French-inspired rooms. To let your favored yellow
shine, pair it with white trim and woodwork.

◆ *above:* Often considered a neutral, bright, sunny yellow balances vibrant reds, blues, and greens. Here, a pretty
medium shade holds its own with the classic red floral and deep-hued, patterned rug—and is a handsome backdrop
for the black sconce shades above the mantel and the mix of collected accessories and framed art.

COLOROPTIONS *Think of pale yellows and yellow-greens as the delicate colors of early spring that warm the
cold earth with the first hints of color. These shades of cheer will likewise warm your home and heart through the year.*

◆ *above:* Paint your walls cheerful, sunshine yellow to brighten a room with little natural light. Happy yellows are guaranteed to lift your decorating spirits. Here, the brick fireplace is painted rusty red to introduce a second dose of strong color. When you use such a strong color, repeat it in fabrics or accessories.

◆ *opposite:* Lovers of bright primary colors can indulge their passion in casual porch and sunporch settings. Rather than pastels or awning stripes, bright red-and-blue floral cushions create a cottage setting. Remember that unmatched tablecloths are more fun than sets—just repeat the dominant colors for a sense of pleasing harmony.

COLOROPTIONS *Find warmth in unexpected places— such as rosy pink and light peach; clear, medium shades of green and lilac keep the scheme from overheating.*

colors for warmth

DECORATING A ROOM WITH A NORTHERN EXPOSURE OR A ROOM WITH LITTLE NATURAL LIGHT? Think about colors that warm your decor and, on cold nights, your soul. Nothing is cheerier than classic yellow as a wall color. Treated as neutrals, pretty, sunny yellows are appropriate in any room of your home. For a cozy, comfortable palette, combine yellow with shades of rusty and clear reds. Red and yellow alone, often supplied by patterned fabrics, are the classic warm palette. Or, if you like the primary scheme of red, yellow, and blue, use cool blue as the supporting player. Remember, too, that texture and pattern contribute to warmth. Introduce wood tones and mixes of prints.

COLOR OPTIONS

shades of green

EVEN WITH THE POPULARITY OF BRIGHT-AND-BOLD LIME AND YELLOW TINTS, GREEN REMAINS A TRADITIONAL COOL-DOWN HUE. A neighbor to blue on the cool side of the color wheel, green "says" outdoors. No artificial palette recreates the variety of nature. Walk outside and look at the trees, grass, ornamental shrubs, flowers, and weeds for the breadth of shades of this calming color. You'll find it all from the darkest blue-greens of evergreens to the palest apple greens. Here's a tip from nature: Greens have a way of blending and working together. Don't worry about precisely matching shades in fabrics, paint, and rugs. As long as you vary the patterns and scale, greens will coexist happily together.

◆ *right:* A shade doesn't have to be intense or dark to be dramatic. Here, the effect is eye-catching as the walls, trim, built-in bunk beds, and even the ladder are all painted in a shade of cool, minty green. Green is the ideal color for this one-stop treatment— calmer than energetic red and warmer than cool blue.

COLOROPTIONS

From interiors to accessories, green is the color of the moment. Dark or light, bright or subtle, use it for walls that reflect the natural calm of nature. Or try jolts of bright green for simple curtains or easy-to-switch accessories.

COLOR OPTIONS

◆ *left:* A silk moiré-style wallcovering and painted trim create a paneled effect for a lively interpretation of a traditional living room. Look for wallcoverings that emulate fabric or decorative finishes as an alternative to solid painted surfaces. Repeat your color—here as the pleated lampshade and velvet bow hanger—to pull a pretty, decorated look together.

◆ *below:* Clear greens, with a touch of yellow for warmth, contrast nicely with the rusty red shades often used for country-style furniture. If you like green in small doses, use it as a trim or door color.

◆ *left:* With nature as your guide, don't hesitate to mix shades of green from the palest to the darkest. To keep the look airy and fresh, mix the classic look of awning stripes with light, painted pieces and natural woods. Remember that weathered greens impart their own charms as the floor-length shutters attest.

◆ *right:* You don't have to paint your walls fire engine red to enjoy the romance of a red room. Instead, use a fabric such as this scenic toile print, which offers the relief of a white background. For most impact, use enough fabric to make a statement—here the bed hanging, coverlet, and window treatment unify the design.

◆ *below:* Brick red warms rooms with dark-painted or stained wood as this kitchen illustrates. In a room with high ceilings and stainless steel, red makes what could be a cold space into a room that's inviting. Not sure of your shade? Paint three swatches on the wall and note how light affects intensity.

red!

NO OTHER COLOR CARRIES THE SYMBOLISM OF POWER AND GLORY THAT RED DOES. Long associated with royalty and celebrations, red connotes energy, excitement, passion, and warmth. Use large doses of red in active, vibrant rooms such as a nighttime dining room or a kitchen for family gatherings. Or cozy up a study or library with a dark, rich shade. Reds range from the cooler purple (burgundy) side of the spectrum to clear, pure brights to warmer brick and lively orange-tinged shades. If too much red overpowers, lighten with white or grayed neutrals for airiness without color competition. As an alternative, consider key decorative accents such as pillows, throws, or lampshades.

◆ *above:* Use the strength of red to establish your design. Here the exterior red door, painted in shiny enamel, hints at the reds to come. Note how the red-white-and-blue-plaid foyer chair sets the stage for the red-and-white dining room visible through the cased opening.

◆ *right:* Known as the color that increases appetite, red is a natural for the dining room. For spark and spunk, choose a semigloss red or apply an extra top layer of shiny glaze.

COLOR*OPTIONS*

From bricks and oranges to cranberries and deep royal purplish hues, reds enliven.

COLOR OPTIONS

living rooms & dining rooms

Look, mood, style, and color preference are the fundamentals of finding a decorative paint finish that enhances your living and dining areas.

Consider how you want your rooms to feel and the colors of your furnishings. If you are updating a room with existing fabrics, you have the option of working with a similar wall color in a fresh technique or starting over with a revised scheme. For example, if your existing walls are yellow, repeat yellow but in a new sponging or striped finish. If you are ready for a change, switch from yellow to terra-cotta in a leather finish.

For the best results when choosing a decorative finish, match the technique to the style of your room. Techniques, such as strié, shown on pages 278–279, which replicate traditional fabrics or wallpapers, provide a backdrop for more formal settings. Other techniques, such as the ever-classic sponging or ragging, work well for a variety of styles. Generally, more loose strokes invite a more informal effect. The trend today for country cottage, and garden-style rooms are the aged techniques, which emulates the effects of time-worn plaster. A smoke-stain technique, shown on pages 270–271, gives an ideal background for country furnishings.

Next, consider how and when you will use a room before you select or change your palette and specific paint colors. If you use a dining room primarily at night with chandelier light or candlelight, think about a darker or more intense shade of your color choice. Look at test swatches at night in artificial light to make sure you are happy with your choices.

If the colors of your foundation furniture or fabrics are dark or vibrant in color in your living room, try balancing the wall color by pulling a shade from their palette to create interest. Or, with your color palette in mind, choose midrange colors of paint for a pleasing, not overpowering appearance. If one shade of color doesn't work with your color scheme, other easy-to-live-with choices can be used in its place. Study the effects of light and relationship to other colors in the room before making a final commitment.

Just remember, color trends come and go, but classic combinations are always in fashion. Whether your style leans more toward contemporary or traditional, with the help of the chapters in this book, you'll find time-honored color schemes and decorative painting techniques that work best for your own personal look.

Balance a colorful, decorative wall finish with the relief of white woodwork and solid upholstery fabric.

◆ **SPONGING,** *opposite,* works well in most settings, depending on how paint is applied and the colors chosen. Decorative painters often adhere to the rule that the looser and more open the sponging, the more casual the look. Here, a persimmon color is densely sponged over a paler background color. The decorator chose the color to blend with the antique rug and the tapestry fabrics. Choose closely related colors to avoid jarring contrasts. **See pages 274–275 for technique.**

living room revivals

NOTHING RESCUES OLDER HOMES—AND FAMILIES ON TIGHT BUDG-ETS—FASTER THAN FRESH PAINT. Here, an existing rug sets the agenda for a vibrant color scheme. In a previous home, the cranberry-and-navy kilim rug anchored a pale terra-cotta room. In a much smaller living room with white-painted grasscloth walls, small windows, and a stone fireplace, the rug dominated (see before). To balance the strong cranberry red, the owners decided to try an equally intense wall color. They taped up paint chips in numerous shades of red, eventually narrowing their choices to three shades. Before making the final commitment, they painted swatches of paint above the sofa and mantel (see left). One red was obviously too rusty, the other too bright. Fortunately, as with the little bear's por-ridge, one stock shade was just right. For extra depth of color, as the room is often used for entertaining at night, they chose a semigloss finish. If you prefer not to call attention to wall texture, such as this painted grasscloth, or to less-than-perfect walls, use flat paint.

◆ *left:* Not ready for a wall test? Paint your choices on poster board and lean or tape in place to study the effects of light on your colors.

◆ *opposite top:* Take advantage of moving as an opportunity to rethink your color choices. Here, a rug that worked fine in another house overpowered this small room. Because of the long, harsh winters, the owners turned to red paint to warm the cool room.

◆ *above:* With the rug balanced by the wall color, the stone fireplace takes its rightful place as the focal point. In soft lamplight, the room glows at night. Such intense color can look harsh with bright ceiling-mounted lighting. If you like overhead light, install a dimmer for control.

◆ **SMOKED STAIN OVER RAGGING OFF,** *above,*
combines two techniques to re-create the look of years
of natural aging. Such aged finishes are a suitable
background for distressed furniture and are popular for
decorating schemes based on country furnishings and
collectibles. **See pages 270–271 for technique.**

◆ **SMOKED STAIN OVER RAGGING OFF,** *right,*
amplifies the earthy colors of country decorating. More
noticeably "stained" areas, created with tinted glaze,
look best where they would naturally occur, such as in
corners between walls and around woodwork
and trim. **See pages 270–271 for technique.**

◆ *Above:* This family room is anchored by a diamond-pattern floor; the fresh treatment helps the room feel cool and breezy in the summer yet cozy in the winter. After the floor is sanded, a diamond pattern is taped off. Alternating diamonds are whitewashed, and small pewter-color squares are painted in the corners. The entire floor is finished with two coats of paste wax to protect the surface from everyday use. **See pages 254–255 for information on creating hand-painted diamonds.**

◆ **SPONGING,** *opposite,* over stippling, doesn't overwhelm a room with deep windows and light carpet and furniture. Stipple first, allow to dry, then sponge. In a room with less light, choose paler shades for the wall. **See pages 262–263, direction A, for stippling techique; see pages 274–275 for sponging technique.**

◆ **GLAZING OVER SPONGED STRIPES,** *opposite,* gives a hand-painted interpretation of classic, striped wallpaper. When art and furniture are the focal points in a room, choose subtle colors from tints on the same paint card. Neutral colors translate well into this stylish, relaxed look. Consider the impact of jewel-tone stripes for a living or dining room used primarily at night. **See pages 242–243 for stripes technique.**

◆ **WIDE STRIPES,** *left,* set an interesting, welcoming tone for a foyer. The finish highlights pieces such as this gilded chair and framed print—and visually expands a small space. Choose colors that blend harmoniously with adjoining rooms. **See pages 242–243 for stripes technique.**

◆ **RAGGING OFF,** *above,* introduces the element of dimension. Paint is rolled on, then removed with rags. The result gives a hint of pleasing texture without competing with collections. Darker shades, as shown here, or lighter tints, can be ragged off. **See pages 270–271 for technique.**

WHEN COUNTRY DECORATING IS YOUR JOY, PERSONALIZE YOUR ROOMS WITH THE CHARM OF STENCILED BORDERS. Since colonial days, stenciled patterns have been prized as economical tools that decorate and add color to rooms. For a fresh, clean version of country-style, combine garden motifs and spring green and sunny yellow fabrics with traditional country furniture and accessories. The combination is charming and easy to emulate.

◆ *upper left:* The botanical slipcover fabric sets the decorating scheme in this country-style parlor. Rather than replicate the fabric's leaf motif, a compatible ginkgo leaf from a commercial stencil graces the light green walls. A vintage secondhand mirror, its distressed frame untouched, reflects the scene.

◆ *lower left:* The meandering vine appears to grow around the plain oak woodwork. The whimsical effect updates the somewhat serious carved settee, an early-20th-century piece.

◆ *opposite:* Detailed by the stenciled gingko leaves, the cased opening captures a view into the adjacent dining room. As a compatible and not competing technique to stenciling, decoratively painted moiré stripes update the furnishings in the dining room. In the living room, an antique grandfather clock and artwork stand out against the stenciled wall. **See page 302 for technique.**

◆ *left:* To emphasize a collection of antique olive oil jars, the deep green stenciled border recalls the classical leaf motifs of Greece and Italy. The dark green gives weight and impact to the stenciled border and balances the deep tones of the jars. A pale-colored stencil would have seemed visually unbalanced.

◆ *below:* A deep shade of pumpkin instantly energizes the dining room. Blackish green paint enriches the crown molding above the stylized border. The placement of the border slightly below the molding makes the ceiling appear higher. A simple, frameless mirror, scenic print, and metal serving stand are unified by the backdrop.

FOR A SOPHISTICATED ACCENT, CONSIDER A TAILORED BORDER COMPATIBLE WITH THE STYLE AND FURNISHINGS OF YOUR ROOM. Position a stenciled border in a living or dining room as you would a wallpaper border—taking into account the background color of the wall as well as art and accessories as you determine the border motif. Deep rich walls, as well as light pale walls, are equally suitable for stenciled borders. The key to choosing interesting paint colors is to ensure sufficient contrast between the border and backdrop. If you decorate an older or a historic-style home, browse through architectural history or period decorating books for stencil pattern ideas.

◆ *opposite:* In an early-20th-century house, the natural simplicity of the stylized leaf-and-berry border complements the Arts and Crafts style of a sitting area enriched with paneled wainscoting. The background warms the setting and lightens the effect of the oak French doors while the stencil introduces pattern and color.

Color-washed neutral colors translate blank walls and ceilings into rooms that relax formal furnishings.

◆ **COLOR-WASHED WITH DILUTED PAINT,** *opposite*, recreates the appeal of old fresco without textured paints or glazes. This popular look ages new construction. Dilute white latex paint with water and color wash the ceiling and walls. Shades of cream and brown soften the effects.

◆ **COLOR WASHED WITH DILUTED PAINT,** *left,* sets the color tones for graceful window treatments in a rich silk fabric. The ceiling could be lightened or darkened to create a more dramatic contrast.

See pages 248–249 for color wash (faded fresco).

◆ **COMBED COLOR WASH AND SPONGING,** *opposite,* takes advantage of the chair rail to combine two treatments. Above the chair rail, the color wash is combed for texture. Below, sponging creates the contrast of wainscoting. The darker color anchors the room. **See pages 248–249 for color wash (faded fresco); pages 244–245 for combing; and pages 274–275 for sponging.**

◆ **TINTED TEXTURED PAINT,** *left,* uses a commercially available paint to recreate the look and feel of stucco. The colors, here warm yellow with tints of ochre, are added to the paint. If you prefer to add visual texture to walls, recreate the look with ragging or ragging off techniques.

◆ **FAUX-TILE FLOOR,** *below,* transforms a small dining area and basic furnishings into a European-inspired setting. To disguise a worn floor, the owners painted a decorative faux-tile motif. With the floor as the anchor of the sunny scheme, walls are color-washed with diluted latex paint in the warm yellows associated with country French colors. When two techniques are combined, keep one simple for a pleasing effect.

See pages 250–251 for faux-tile technique; see pages 248–249 for color wash (faded fresco).

◆ **STRIPES (FLAT PAINT),** *above,*
introduce variations of neutral color into a
monochromatic, contemporary dining
room. Stripes warm such serene rooms
without the impact of vivid color or busy
pattern. The color blends with the carpet
and the natural wood furniture. If you
prefer more contrast between stripes, paint
semigloss stripes over a flat wall finish.
Or choose the lightest and darkest colors
on a paint chip card. Two- to three-inch-
wide stripes are a pleasing scale for
average-size dining or living rooms.
See pages 242–243 for stripes technique.

◆ **SPONGED STRIPES,** *above,* create the illusion of higher ceiling height. Here, the verticality of the stripes combine with the window treatments hung below the molding to give a standard dining room an open, airy feel. To make a room feel larger, choose light colors with a noticeable, but not pronounced, contrast between the stripes.

Decide which element in your room will be the star. The quiet wall colors allow the antique rug and the chandelier to be the decorating focal points. **See pages 242–243 for stripes technique; see pages 274–275 for sponging technique.**

◆ **RANDOM COMBING,** *above,* demonstrates the impact of a well-chosen finish for a contemporary interior. The aubergine color imparts drama that's heightened by the random combing. The color and pattern effectively frame the graphic prints. The best rule to follow when color and technique are involved? The more dramatic the color, the simpler the finish. **See pages 264–265 for combing (moiré stripes) technique; see pages 244–245 for standard combing technique.**

◆ **MOIRÉ STRIPES,** *opposite*, update the dining room and its country oak pieces with lively color and pattern. When you plan to work with multiple paint techniques, choose one to stand out so your rooms don't compete with each other. Painted stripes enrich with the look of texture and pattern and are ideal for rooms where the walls can be the decorative stars. **See pages 264–265 for technique.**

◆ **MOIRÉ STRIPES,** above *left,* are an example of how an interesting technique can invigorate a collection of vintage furniture and art. **See pages 264–265 for technique.**

◆ **MOIRÉ STRIPES,** above *center and right,* were chosen to work with the colors and textures of the owner's table linens, glassware, and collections. When you plan a color scheme and complementary technique, consider how your backdrop will reflect your furnishings. Here, the texture highlights collected pottery, while the wide stripe reinforces the solid feel of the country oak furniture. **See pages 264–265 for technique.**

◆ **STENCIL,** *left*: The curved arms of the iron chandelier inspire the simple stencil motif for the two borders and the embellished slipcovers. The red wall color sets off the gold-tone metallic paint used for the recurring stencil. For a pleasing composition, the upper border aligns slightly below the wall niche, while the lower border is at chair-rail height. The motif repeats on cotton slipcover fabric, which absorbs latex paint.

◆ **STENCIL,** *below:* Metallic paint, transforms a repetitive stencil motif into a decorative border. The rich gold reinforces the sheen of the mirror's double frame to unify the dining room. Gold-tone paint adds sparkle and glamorous touches to elevate the look of furnishings in such areas as dining rooms, which are often used at night and for entertaining. Simple motifs work best when the paint color is the star. **See page 286 for technique and page 312 for stencil pattern.**

◆ *above*: An easily accomplished distressed technique unifies an oak table—a flea market bargain because of its damaged top—and four European country-style unfinished chairs. Primer is allowed to soak into the unfinished wood, causing a slightly pickled effect that allows some grain to show. The paint and chairs transform a country table into a sophisticated grouping. **See page 288 for techniques.**

◆ *left*: The sturdy curves of the chair, typical of 19th-century European country furniture, are compatible with the American oak table. The proliferation of well-made unfinished furniture makes it easy to mix new and vintage pieces with the artistry of paint.

ENRICH YOUR DINING ROOM BY PAINTING ONE OR TWO KEY
PIECES TO IMPART FRENCH CHARM. In this era of personal
decorating, consider painting an interesting piece you own, or shop for
vintage or unfinished pieces that would work in the style and scale of
your existing furnishings. As a starting point, look to elements that you
already own, such as wallpaper, rugs, or a collection. Choose pieces that
complement rather than match existing pieces in the room. Finding your
personal style will be fun and rewarding.

◆ *above and right:* Originally too dark for a French-style room, detailed blue
sideboard, now adds buoyancy to the traditional-style dining room. Wallpaper,
porcelains, and the rug inspired the colors. Deep drawers and sturdy construction
make it ideal for linen and flatware storage. **See page 290 for techniques.**

bedrooms & bathrooms

Bedrooms more than ever, should be spaces of comfort and havens of rest—ideal places to calm down or spice up with special paint finishes.

To make a bedroom and bath your own, choose a paint technique and color scheme that reflects your taste and furnishings. Bedrooms can be adorned in the softest sponging to the newer techniques that emulate fabrics, suede, and leathers. Stripes, diamonds, or hand-painted squares are options for spirited, up-to-date looks.

Children's rooms and nurseries are the perfect venue for creativity and imagination. Painted in stylish soft pastels, or bold stripes and patterns, walls and furniture can transform lighthearted backgrounds into works of art that accentuate existing surroundings. Or, if you are feeling a bit daring, try your hand at easy freehand designs and the use of decorative stencils that allow you to choose your own patterns and colors.

Bathrooms, although usually small in size, can be brought to life instantly with color and painted patterns and become a focal point from adjoining rooms.

So, whether you are new to decorative painting or a stylish pro, bedrooms and bathrooms are an ideal canvas for experimenting. You'll enjoy the excitement and sense of accomplishment decorative painting can provide.

Ice Blue and Warm Gray

French Vanilla and Almond

Pale Blue and Blush

Terra-Cotta and Sable

Honey Wheat and Olive

Metallics and Ochre

Cool Gray and Barely Beige

restful retreats

WHEN YOU DESIRE CALM, LIMIT COLOR FOR A SOOTHING ENVIRONMENT WITHOUT THE VISUAL EXCITEMENT OF BRIGHT SHADES OR VIVID PATTERNS. Neutrals usually refer to the "noncolors" shown here with black as an accent. Monochromatic schemes are variations of one color, which may or may not be neutral. Neutrals create interest in their own right, relying on texture and subtle variation, rather than the instant impact of color. Light accent colors are often part of the scheme.

◆ Sophisticated and soothing, this bedroom employs a mix of subtle patterns, fabrics, and furnishings for interest. Use painted and distressed finishes as well as informal accessories, such as the quilt, to relax formal furnishings and monochromatic schemes.

Choose paint colors and techniques that unify your existing furnishings and enhance the decorating look you enjoy. Softer colors and simple finishes relax bedroom schemes.

◆ **STRIPES,** *opposite,* relax the formality of decorative French-style furniture. For a lighthearted feel, visually "tent" the ceiling with hand-painted stripes. Choose soft, subtle colors with minimal contrast. **See pages 242–243 for technique.**

◆ **STRIPES,** *above,* fit the corners and angles of attic-like spaces. Think blending, rather than exactly matching colors, when you are pairing painted stripes with painted furniture and cheerfully printed floral fabrics. **See pages 242–243 for technique.**

◆ **CHECKERBOARD,** *below*, updates a worn wood floor in an attic bedroom. Depending on your preference, tape the painted floor for squares as shown, or turn squares at a 45-degree angle for a diamond pattern. Choose the floor colors and finishes to be compatible with the walls and furnishings of your bedroom. To visually anchor a room, select a darker shade of the wall color for one of the floor colors. The contrasting color can be the white, off-white, or stained wood, as shown here, depending on your scheme and preference. Painted floors should always be finished with matte-finish polyurethane to stand up to normal wear. **See pages 238–241 for technique.**

◆ *above*: Begin with a small, easy-to-paint room, such as this decoratively painted bath. A single sponging technique in a pale neutral tone sets off the use of white trims, linens, and window coverings.

EMULATE THE ALWAYS CHIC WHITE-ON-WHITE
ROMANTIC PRESENCE WITH A CAREFULLY STYLED
BEDROOM THAT MINIMIZES COLOR WHILE
EMPHASIZING DETAILS. Turn to such a soothing
scheme when your goal is to create a relaxing,
composed retreat.

◆ *above:* Based on a vintage bed and armoire, both
cleaned up and refreshed with paint, the bedroom
derives its charm from the color and pattern discipline.
Carpet and bed linens contribute texture without a

distracting, obvious pattern; the sheers soften and diffuse light while lending an ethereal atmosphere to the room. In keeping with the minimalist color approach, a painted pressed-tin fragment hangs above the bed, and a collection of oval platters artfully introduces diverse shapes. Silver-tone lamps pair with white silk lampshades, offering subtle contrast yet following the no-color rule.

◆ *above left and opposite below:* Previously painted or antiqued furniture, such as the inherited armoire, may require only cleaning and updated hardware to make a dramatic appearance
in a room of painted furniture.

◆ *above right:* A budget-stretching bookcase fits smartly into the chic setting courtesy of fresh white paint. It provides an ideal backdrop for a collection of old and new white vases, chosen for shapes and mixed with white-jacketed books. Books also can be covered with white paper, with artfully handwritten titles on the jacket spines.

◆ *left:* Previously antiqued, this handsome vintage bed is revived with careful cleaning followed by touching up the detailing with paint. When furniture includes similar adornment, avoid multiple coats of paint that may obscure intricate motifs. **See page 294 for techniques.**

◆ **SPONGING,** *above,* tints a plain wall with hints of warm color. As with ragging, the looser the sponging, the more informal the look and feel of a room. Here, in a country-style room, walls are loosely sponged as a backdrop to painted woodwork and colorful fabrics.

As the vintage fabrics, rug, and furnishings set the scheme, the sponging gives subtle contrast but is a background player. Choose techniques and colors that enhance, rather than overwhelm, your room. **See pages 274–275 for sponging technique.**

SPONGING, *left,* introduces soft shades of creamy white into a pretty yellow bedroom. Lightly sponge in colors from the same paint chip card to avoid harsh contrast. Choose yellows and warm pinks when you want a warm, cozy feel. If you prefer a cool, serene retreat, sponge in shades of cool, pale blue or in lighter greens. Subtle sponging with a natural sponge contributes a quiet background that works with a variety of fabrics, such as the woven tapestry shown here. **See pages 274–275 for technique.**

◆ **LARGE DIAMOND PATTERN (PAINTED),** *above,* lends a sophisticated air to rooms decorated with contemporary furniture and art. When furniture is in simple, graphic shapes, choose oversize diamonds to avoid too much pattern or unsettling contrast. Soft colors can be distressed with a color wash to age the look. Measure so that diamonds are properly spaced. Consider the technique for a focal-point wall, rather than an entire room. Paint adjoining walls in one of the colors. **See pages 260–261 for diamond technique.**

◆ *above:* Bold stripes created with painter's tape and two shades of paint transform a vintage 1920s-era chest into a handsome traditional room accent. Gold- and silver-tone paint defines the chest and emphasizes the delicately turned legs on this period piece.

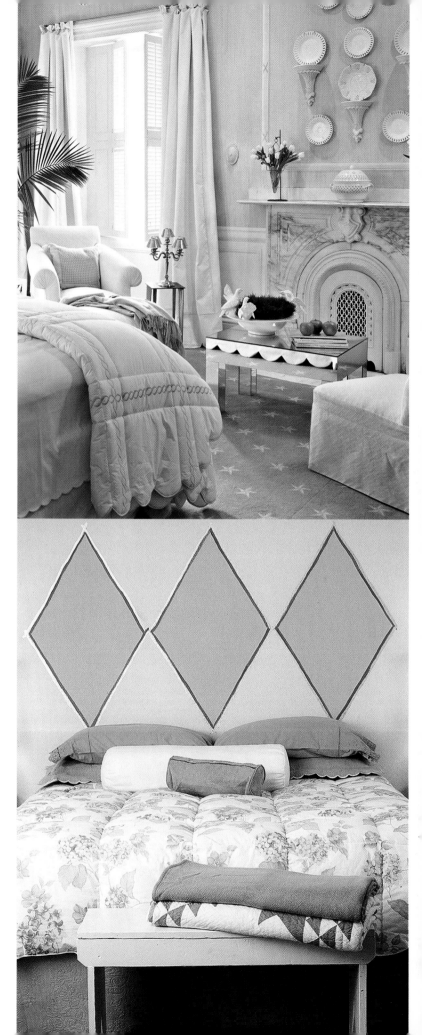

◆ **COMBING,** *top right*, refines the background in a room of icy pastels. The texture contrasts with the smoothness of collected white porcelains that are arranged and hung as art. Such combed finishes can be used effectively above wainscoting, as shown, for the effect of wallpaper. Lighter wall colors introduce a feeling of summer when combined with white woodwork and white or pale fabrics. **See pages 244–245 for combing technique.**

◆ **LARGE-SCALE DIAMOND PATTERN,** *lower right,* hand-painted diamonds in a repeated row are perfect for romantic settings, as in this bedroom. The three diamonds run the width of the bed, creating the look of a headboard and giving the treatment focal-point status. **See pages 260-261 for this technique.**

◆ **FULL WALL OF DIAMONDS,** *opposite,* neatly mapped out across the wall with softly painted lines, these outlined diamonds link together for an elegant look of tufted fabric. The buttons painted at every point emphasize the three-dimentional look. Repeated on the fabulous painted furniture, the diamond pattern is a cohesive motif for the room. **See pages 260–261 for diamond technique.**

◆ *right:* An old oak dresser takes on a lighter, more sophisticated air with a lightly distressed white paint finish. To echo the mirror, the curved drawer fronts are stenciled with a shell design, that traditionally has been carved into furniture. A white shade on the candlestick-style lamp and silver accessories complete the charming arrangement.

◆ *below:* Echoing the delicate wall stencils, a discreet ribbon trellis in two soft shades decorates the top of a painted chest. This minimal color sets a chic, yet romantic mood for a bedroom. Furniture can be sealed with a matte-finish polyurethane to prevent chipping and undue wear.

◆ *opposite:* Delicately glazed and stenciled walls create a springtime background for an old iron bed and oak dresser, both freshened with white paint. In the essence of a garden arbor, the background stencil depicts a ribbon trellis, while green glaze softens the effect. The trellis pattern comes to life with an overlay of a stenciled wisteria vine in full bloom. The vine cascades in subtle detailing between the iron bed and the painted dresser. This garden wall scene turns a small bedroom into a pretty, serene setting. The coverlet and sham in a delicate wisteria print enhance the airy garden mood. The plaid accent pillow, piped in a fresh green, repeats the lavender and green of the two-color palette and contributes a pleasing round shape. The quilt emphasizes the old-fashioned garden theme without the distraction of additional color or pattern.

◆ **STRIPES,** *above left,* illustrate the pretty, always-classic color combination of blue and white. Here, the blue is a cool, stylish periwinkle that lends itself well to a teenager's bedroom. The stripes provide a lively counterpoint to the woven coverlet hung as art above the bed. A horizontal, pleated window treatment adds the design interest of contrasting lines. When a room is likely to change, choose such classic color combinations and decorative techniques. The versatile striped walls, which seem old-fashioned with the mix of vintage furnishings, fabrics, and white wicker, could feel equally sporty or contemporary with a quick change of furniture, linens, and window treatments. **See pages 242–243 for stripes technique.**

◆ **STRIPES,** *above center,* take on a sophisticated, grown-up flair in a luxurious master bedroom. For this look, choose two shades of rich gold that blend with an equally opulent woven fabric for the padded, shirred headboard and duvet cover. The repetition of colors in the painted stripes and fabrics enriches the setting. For a cooler look, decorate with shades of silver, off-white, or pale tans. **See pages 242–243 for stripes technique.**

◆ **COLOR BLOCK STRIPES,** *above right,* perk up a small guest room with wide bands of copper-color textured paint, tempered by two colors of flat green paint. First, paint the walls with the lightest color of flat paint; then mark off stripes with a level and straightedge; pencil in guidelines. Mask off and roll on the bands of the darker flat paint; allow to dry. Mask off and roll on textured paint. Stripes here are 6, 12, 18, and 30 inches wide. Purchase the sand-textured paint at home centers and larger paint stores. For the most effective backdrop, choose colors of noticeable contrast but with similar brightness, as shown here. Two neutral colors from the same paint card pair well with a more dramatic color.

IF LATE 19TH- OR EARLY 20TH-CENTURY FURNITURE SEEMS TOO DARK OR HEAVY FOR YOUR DECOR, BRING IT INTO THE 21ST CENTURY WITH FRESH WHITE PAINT. (Keep in mind that painting a valuable antique lowers its value. If you think a piece is an authentic antique, check with a reputable dealer before painting or altering its finish.) As you shop for bargain pieces to paint, look for furniture that has interesting trim or detailing that will highlight well with paint. Disregard dated fabrics on chair backs and seats. Contemporary fabrics, in lively 21st-century colors, provide the final transformation. For the best results, always sand and prime stained or painted pieces. Choose a shade of white or cream that works with your wall colors, fabrics, and accessories.

◆ *opposite:* A creamy shade of white enamel lightens and brightens a previously dark-stained dresser and a pair of flea market dining chairs. Even the country-style shelf bracket is painted to coordinate with the lighthearted, cheerful setting.

◆ *below:* Designers are transforming dark Eastlake-style furniture into fashionable accent pieces with white paint and fabrics. The hall table and straight chair, classic Eastlake pieces, stand out against a sunny yellow background.

◆ *top right:* Painted white and then antiqued, an inherited hall table and mirror provide ample background for a prized 19th-century dresser bowl and water pitcher.

◆*below right:* White paint updates early 20th-century furniture for a cheerful setting that welcomes guests. Floral fabric contribute to the airy appeal.

An expanded interest in European styles translates into new reproduction furniture collections. Observe these pieces, *above*, to discover painted pieces that match your style. Rather than hold fast to only one furnituremaker, mix similarly finished pieces to achieve the one-of-a-kind look that comes from incorporating antiques and family treasures. Pair thrift store pieces with new or painted pieces. When you don't find the perfect country piece to complete your setting, create your own heirloom with paint and traditional motifs applied to a headboard, chest, or bedside table.

◆ *below and below right:* The custom-designed headboard sports the most personal of motifs—a couple's hand-painted, combined monogram. Although a woodworking shop cut the featured headboard from ¾-inch plywood, an unfinished or secondhand store headboard would serve as well for this embellishment. A glazed finish over the painted headboard mellows the appearance and blends with the tones of the fern-printed fabric. Repeating the muted green found in the yellow-green tints of the print unifies the decorating scheme. The white coverlet and shams and the subtly striped sheets allow the painted and glazed headboard to play the starring role. As an alternative, one initial could be painted, or a monogram or an initial could be stenciled and softened with hand-painted accents. **See page 289 for techniques.**

◆ *right:* An antiqued, glazed finish rejuvenates a dated metal tray table for a useful and attractive accent piece for a bath. The lip and the tray handles make the piece functional for grouping bath items and accessories. Small trays such as this also work well in the living room or family room as drink or magazine tables. Here, the muted colors and finishes echo the sophisticated tone of a white bath. Cutouts could also be decoupaged on the tabletop and sealed with polyurethane. **See page 294 for techniques.**

LET YOUR IMAGINATION RUN WILD AND DESIGN A ROOM TARGETED TO YOUR CHILD'S INTERESTS AND LOVES. If your son or daughter has a favorite animal, such as the mischievous monkey featured here, you've found a fun starting point. Look for a commercial stencil or stencils in your theme—or find a fabric that can be simplified for a custom stencil. Work with colors appropriate for the animal and its background so your young naturalist can feel part of the habitat.

◆ *right:* Warm, natural colors are an appropriate setting for the monkey and the jungle of this boy's room. A jungle-theme-printed fabric translates into duvet covers for the bunk beds. Natural bamboo blinds contribute an appropriate window treatment while guaranteeing privacy and sun control. Wall-mounted baskets neatly corral playful monkeys and other stuffed animals, while a larger wicker basket serves as a perfect toy hamper. The dark red desk and bookcase and green chair repeat colors from the stenciled red balls and the foliage.

◆ *above:* Although he frolics in a jungle setting, this fun-loving monkey with a red ball in each paw obviously has visited the circus. Stenciled details, added as an overlay, create his quizzical expression. To further replicate the jungle theme, palm fronds are cut from sponges and stamped on the hand-painted vines. Two shades of green paint, some lightly stamped, enhance the natural appearance of the fronds. **See pages 304–305 for technique and pages 314–315 for patterns.**

CREATE A ROOM A YOUNG GIRL WILL GROW INTO
RATHER THAN OUT OF. If you change accessories as
the years pass, the delicately detailed painted furniture in this pastel room will charm her well into
her teen years.

◆   *above:* A well-chosen paint scheme unifies and
updates unmatched furniture. The single bed, dresser,
and straight chair—all assorted flea market finds—
appear made for the armoire, which was purchased
unfinished. The secret to success is to work with pieces
of similar scale and style and to repeat detailing and

colors from piece to piece. Here, outlining with blue
enlivens and coordinates the room without
overpowering it. **See pages 296–297 for techniques.**

◆   *above and opposite:* Stripes on the walls, created
with painter's tape, along with a painted peg rack,
animate a room full of fresh pastels and youthful
fabrics. Mixing pastels, patterns, cool blues and greens,
tailored stripes, the lush bed hanging, and the chain-
stitched floral rug conveys grown-up direction. The
mosaic-framed mirror adds an exotic touch to the
teapots, teacups, and floral plates.

◆ *above:* A hand-painted ribbon motif decorates the doors of the armoire detailed with old-fashioned glass knobs. Stenciled motifs or wallpaper could be used as alternatives, or the doors could be painted to contrast with one of the colors used in the room. **See page 297 for techniques.**

◆ *left:* Soft casual touches bring the scene together. Wide stripes on the lampshade reflect the wall treatment. **See page 296 for techniques.**

REFRESH A BEDROOM WITH A FLORAL THEME TRANSLATED FROM FASHIONABLE APPLIQUÉD SHEER FABRIC. The springtime look adapts well for a young girl's room, as shown—or with different furnishings and accessories for a romantic adult bedroom. Start with hand-painted stripes, in cool blue and green, as a tailored background for tulips that are created with commercial stencils. With the popularity of sheer fabrics and ready-made sheer drapery panels, it's easy to find flowers and motifs to set your theme.

◆ *left:* Paired with stripes, stenciled tulips update a small upstairs bedroom. Tulips repeat on the painted and stenciled, scalloped-edge floorcloth to neatly unify the decorating scheme. The balance of white, from the narrow stripes and ceiling to the furniture, brightens and visually expands the room. White paint also works magic in updating a dark spindle bed to work with traditional white wicker. A new chenille bedspread, woven in classic style, and crisp linens dress the bed.

◆ *above left:* A light pouncing motion gives stenciled tulips a charming hand-painted look in the style of botanical art. The commercial stencil features softer lines and more detailing than the appliqué tulip and is compatible with the folk art look. The two-color scheme with blue tulips transforms a traditional motif into a stylish setting.

◆ *above right:* Floorcloth fabric cut into an oval scalloped rug provides a smooth, sturdy surface for a painted background and stenciled tulips. Repeating the color scheme of the striped walls, two tulip motifs are stenciled inside the painted border to add appealing decorative interest. A polyurethane sealer on the floorcloth ensures long wear and continued beauty. **See page 283 for technique.**

GIVE MISMATCHED FLEA MARKET FINDS OR INHER-ITED FURNITURE NEW LIFE WITH AN ARTFUL ARRAY OF CANDY-BOX PASTELS. Recall the colors of dinner mints—and for the liveliest mix, collect paint chips of your favorite pastels plus white. Choose colors of the same intensity or degree of brightness—generally in corresponding locations on paint chips—to avoid a bright yellow, for example, overpowering a pale green.

◆ *right:* A patchwork quilt inspires the delicate pastel color scheme for this girl's room. The flea market lamp table goes from staid to lively with a bright white top and light yellow base. **See page 298 for techniques.**

◆ *below and below right:* A dressing table, with applied detailing, is pretty in pink while the chair is lively in yellow and white. White unifies the mix of pastels and pieces. **See page 298 for techniques.**

◆ *below left:* The curved drawer fronts and scalloped apron of this early-20th-century chest lend themselves to the delicacy of soft green and white. The white top introduces a crisp, contemporary air and repeats on each piece for pleasing design unity. Although this chest is an inherited family piece, look for similar ones at vintage furniture stores, flea markets, or tag sales. Older stained or painted pieces should be cleaned, repaired, sanded, and primed before painting in order for the paint to adhere.

◆ *below:* New hardware, such as these clear cut-glass knobs, purchased from a home furnishings catalog, stylishly updates vintage chests, dressing tables, desks, and wardrobes. In keeping with the pastel scheme inspired by a patchwork quilt, walls are washed in a soft blue as a backdrop for the painted furniture. The furniture trim allows each painted piece to stand out against the background. The coordinating decorative shelf displays a framed pastel print, while the small accent lamp, gingham lampshade, and a child's painted china tea set add pretty finishing touches to a room that will grow along with the little one. **See page 298 for technique.**

◆ *opposite:* Fashionable imported sheer fabric with appliquéd flowers and vines combined with a pretty shade of periwinkle blue inspire this bedroom designed for a teenage girl. The cool shade plus the crisp white illustrate the strong design and youthful sophistication of a carefully edited scheme. Stenciled white flowers and vines embellish periwinkle walls, while periwinkle flowers enliven white fabrics. White flowers on sheer fabric cover periwinkle accent pillows. The white feather-boa-style lamp and white accent pillows add the finishing feminine touches to the pretty scheme.

◆ *top left:* Plain surfaces, such as the window treatment cornice, provide balance in rooms decorated with stenciled motifs. When an eye-catching border receives the attention, plain surfaces provide the necessary balance. For impact at ceiling height, the border flower size is enlarged from the fabric.

◆ *bottom:* Stenciled flowers and vines from the same pattern transform plain white cotton fabric into a beautifully detailed duvet cover and oversize pillow sham. To exactly match the walls, the same periwinkle latex paint is used for the stenciled flowers. For polished decorating touches, pillows wrapped in the sheer fabric are detailed with tailored piping, and the larger accent pillow sports a ruffled trim. **See page 285 for technique and page 316 for stencil patterns.**

WHEN YOU LOVE THE GARDEN, BRING IN THE OUTDOORS FOR YOUR BABY OR TODDLER. With a combination of hand painting and stenciling, you can create a cheerful room that will be fun and stimulating throughout the preschool years.

◆ *opposite:* The garden nursery owes its charm to the overscaled flowers and the soft painterly effects achieved by glaze and sea sponges. For the picket fence, self-adhesive paper, drawn and cut as pickets, covers the original white walls. When the self-adhesive paper is removed, the charming fence remains. The hand-painted bird and birdhouse personalize the scene.

◆ *above left:* Vegetable stencils and hand-painted details animate the painted chest for a distinctive furniture piece. The drapery tieback, cut from plywood and painted, adds a jaunty touch. Even a butterfly gets into the act in a stenciled motif.

◆ *above right:* The hand-painted bunny leaps over stenciled vegetables as a wall detail. The freehand painting and detailing soften the stenciled effect and imbue the room with whimsical, folk art charm. The stenciled pillow decorates a vintage rocker that has been freshened with crisp white paint.

◆ *left:* A neatly stenciled ladybug lights on a stylized flower —just one of the charming, lighthearted details in this room.

See page 301 for technique and page 313 for patterns.

Revive dated furniture with fresh colors and themes that reflect your getaway fantasies.

FREE YOUR IMAGINATION TO FANTASIZE ABOUT THE BED-ROOM OF YOUR DREAMS. For inspiration, give in to your image of an ideal place to live or vacation. For added guidance, spend time with memorable photo albums or glance through travel books, magazines, and websites of enticing, faraway places.

As you browse, visualize colors that soothe and calm you. On the practical side, consider which existing furniture has possibilities of taking on a more exotic life with paint and detailing. When you need to add furniture to your bedroom, shop for vintage or reproduction beds or chests that provide the qualities of charm and history while reflecting your travel longings.

◆ *right:* A summer vacation in Paris and the love for all things French meld into the idea for the palette and cheerfully stylized painted motifs. This project also updates two basic mid-20th-century family pass-along pieces. For lighthearted appeal, the bed and chest both feature the recognizable lively harlequin pattern in tints of lavender and apple green. The medium-tint lavender is repeated in the fresh and cool wall color, as well as in the detail on a previously stained bed. Making the definitive French accent, an artist has hand-painted sketches of the best known of all Paris landmarks—the Eiffel Tower. Three fleur-de-lis tiebacks, cut from plywood and hand-painted, support the bed hanging that matches the drapery panels. The result: a perfect retreat for an American in Paris.

See page 292 for techniques.

◆ *opposite:* The wonderfully bright duvet and sham, with motifs designed to emulate hand-painted fabric, set the style and color scheme for this teenage girl's room. Bright pink and blue leaves, positioned as though they are drifting from a tree, are casually stamped on the white wall. After the leaves are outlined, a brushed-on coat of bright green glaze energizes the scheme with upbeat, youthful color. The white iron bed contributes an interesting shape, and the open design allows the wall to stand out. As an alternative, a wooden bed or pair of twin beds could be painted crisp white or snappy colors that complement the decorating scheme.

◆ *above left:* Graphic shapes echo the motifs and colors of the stamped bedroom walls. The pink tulip lamp on the yellow-skirted table recalls the popular "flower power" look of the 1960s, in vogue again. With vibrant, playful walls and fabrics, a minimum of accessories works best. No wall art is needed as the stamped walls become the engaging art. For another decorating option, one wall could be stamped and the other three glazed in the green.

◆ *above right:* With colorful stamped and glazed walls as the focal point, other design elements, such as the piped seat cushion and accent pillows, naturally play off the scheme. The stamped walls and duvet fabric provide lively pattern while the solid cotton duck pillows balance with visual relief that doesn't distract. The blue piping repeats the blue in the duvet fabric and stamped leaves. **See page 284 for technique and page 312 for stencil patterns.**

◆ **FLOWER BORDER,** *below left,* decorates a young girl's attic-style bedroom with a happy, 1960's-inspired daisy motif. Select lively, fresh colors to have fun with such easy, freehand techniques. The secret to the look is carefully taping and measuring the border and casually brushing on the background. **See pages 252–253 for technique.**

◆ **TAPED STRIPES,** *below right,* give a crisp, youthful background to painted furniture when a vivid green pairs with bright white. **See pages 242–243 for technique.**

◆ **FLOWER BORDER,** *opposite top,* repeats the stylized daisy motif of the duvet cover. Look for such graphic motifs that can be translated into hand-painted borders. The naive, less-than-perfect look contributes to the charm of hand painting. Borders decorate a room without the time and expense of an overall wall technique. Paint trim in one of the border colors. **See pages 252–253 for technique.**

◆ **TAPED STRIPES,** *opposite bottom,* tent a girl's room in circus style. Wider stripes, here 3 inches, lend an informal, playful air to a bedroom. Base your stripe color on a fabric or other color in your room. Here, a cotton chair slipcover inspires the lively, stylish green paired with always-crisp white. For a softer look with stripes, decorate with two shades of yellow or a pale yellow and cream. **See pages 242–243 for technique.**

UNLEASH YOUR CREATIVITY AND ENERGIZE A NURSERY OR TODDLER'S ROOM WITH PRIMARY COLORS TRANS-
LATED INTO A CHEERFUL DOG-AND-CAT THEME. Start with lively, hand-painted stripes as a whimsical background for the fun of framed pet portraits and framed icons of the pet world. Make sure the playful mood
continues by extending the theme with painted and stenciled furniture, themed pillows, and window
treatments detailed with stenciled dog bones.

◆ *above:* Brimming with energy, the engaging nursery combines bright colors and strong graphic shapes into an
appealing theme. The basic shapes and stylized motifs, in crayon colors, recall the storybooks beloved by generations of

young children. To keep the action rolling, the striped wall and shade pair with the painted trim of the stenciled toy chest. Repetition of bright colors unifies the scheme. Vibrant bright red accents transform the window casings and frames into focal points. While the classic white bed gives relief in the colorful milieu, the tailored bumper pad and mattress cover feature the combination of acid green and dark blue. A fashion-conscious baby or curious toddler will be quite at home in such a stylish and visually stimulating setting.

◆ *above:* A vintage wicker chair joins the show with the addition of a red-and-white check cushion and green pillow embellished with stenciled bones. Bones also grace the top of the window cornice, finished neatly with a scalloped edge and fabric-covered red buttons. **See page 301 for technique.**

IF THE OLD WEST FEEDS YOUR CHILD'S SENSE OF HISTORY AND ADVENTURE, CREATE THE PERFECT HOME ON THE RANGE (OR RANCH) WITH A FANTASY BEDROOM. Use painted and decoupaged storage pieces as eye-catching focal points. Warm the cowboy-theme fabrics, accessories, and vintage finds with clever details that reflect your child's interests.

◆ *below and opposite:* A cowboy-motif rug and decoratively painted bricks set the stage for a crackle-drawer chest and a fire engine red cupboard. Horseshoes, lone stars, hide-covered accessories, iron lamp bases, woven blankets, and a wagon wheel contribute to the appeal.

◆ *right:* The dark crackle drawer insets imitate leather and contrast with the light crackle finish. **See page 293 for techniques.** A reproduction cowboy-print fabric covers the invitingly comfortable chair.

◆ *above and left:* Decoupaged prints add Old West scenes to the painted armoire, a vintage find. Decorative painting lightly ages the door and blends it with the painted walls. The cowhide-covered footstool looks at home in this room where furniture and accessories contribute to the theme while providing function. Jackets hang from rustic star hooks, well-worn cowboy boots present an organized display, and a refurbished trunk neatly stores toys. A new trunk, finished to look rustic with either a lighter-weight lid or opening side door, would be safer for little fingers.

◆ *left:* Classic Western adventures, such as the famous Lewis and Clark expedition, embellish the doors of the painted armoire. Art supply and crafts stores are good places to find prints and posters suitable for decoupaging. You can also stencil or stamp simple motifs.

See page 296 for techniques.

EXPAND YOUR CHILD'S HORIZONS WITH A ROOM INSPIRED BY CULTURES NEAR AND FAR. Rather than focusing strictly on one theme or country, create a backdrop for motifs, colors, and furnishings of diverse countries and continents. As a starting point, think about what countries and cultures are of particular interest to your child, perhaps those found in your family heritage, or a favorite school geography project. Look for existing furnishings that can be updated with paint, hardware, and detailing.

◆ *above:* Refreshed with black enamel, an iron metal bed anchors a room of exotic finishes and exotic furnishings. A faux zebra-skin rug repeats the effectiveness of black and white.

◆ *opposite, lower left:* With a nod to design influences from Native American and Asian cultures, stylized geometric motifs detail the painted chest. Stained wooden knobs contrast with orange-red and white. **See page 300 for techniques.** The hammered silver mirror frame adds another exotic touch.

IF YOUR CHILD IS A JUNIOR PALEONTOLOGIST, INDULGE THIS SCIENTIFIC INTEREST WITH A ROOM WHERE THE DINOSAUR REIGNS SUPREME. While these prehistoric creatures are enjoying an all-time popularity, it's easy to find bedding, accessories, and stencils.

◆ *above right:* Hand-painted to suggest geological layers, a basic plywood headboard fastens to the glazed green wall. The headboard could be one color for a simple yet colorful treatment.

◆ *right:* Five of the headboard colors are repeated on the toy chest, which was purchased unfinished. The chest is further personalized with a stenciled and hand-detailed dinosaur. **See page 299 for techniques and page 316 for stencil pattern.**

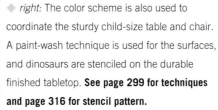

◆ *right:* The color scheme is also used to coordinate the sturdy child-size table and chair. A paint-wash technique is used for the surfaces, and dinosaurs are stenciled on the durable finished tabletop. **See page 299 for techniques and page 316 for stencil pattern.**

Paint—and jaunty stripes—dress up baths whether your style is budget-conscious, country casual, or sleek contemporary.

◆ **STRIPES,** *above,* energize a small, remodeled bath with cheerful yellow and creamy off-white. The look here is casual and hand-painted, rather than precise, to meld with the relaxed charm of the distressed, recycled vanity and vintage linens. (Try it for a child's room, too.) Semigloss paint works well for baths, as it resists moisture and is easier than flat finishes to clean. **See pages 256–257 for technique.**

◆ **FAUX-TILE WALL,** *left,* derives its charm from the freehand, painterly look. This lively scheme, based on 4-inch-square tiles, works well for children's bathrooms as it's playful and youthful but not babyish. An easy-to-choose combination pairs two colors, such as the blue and green shown here, that are near each other on the color wheel. If you prefer the dynamic mixing of opposites, such as orange and blue, choose colors of the same intensities (degree of brightness).

◆ **STENCILED COLOR BLOCKS,** *right,* update an old-fashioned bath with plain white walls. The technique involves a quick combination of cut-out poster board stencil, stencil adhesive to hold it in place, and spray paint. Cutouts are 3 inches square. For the most decorating impact, choose a lively accent color and repeat it in a key accent, such as the painted chair, and in bath linens. For a child's bath, a combination of primary colors or spirited pastels would be a fun and cheerful alternative.

DECORATE A BATH QUICKLY AND ECONOMICALLY WITH STYLISH DOUBLE-STAMPED LEAVES. Use this easy technique as an alternative to wallpaper for detailing all four walls or as an accent wall in a bath or powder room. For a garden-fresh look, start with a fresh coat of light paint, such as pale yellow. To ensure a soft natural look, choose soft shades of green and yellow for the leaves. Restrict accessories to white and natural tones for a nature-oriented theme. As an alternative, work in the rich colors of fall foliage with an earthy terra-cotta or taupe for the background and rich reds and browns for the stamped leaves.

◆ *above:* The casual placement of the leaves to emulate gently blowing breezes heightens the charm and style of stamping. Leaves are in a blending, yet contrasting, shade so that they are clearly visible. Uncomplicated double stamping—a yellow tint stamped over previously stamped green leaves—softens for a serene, natural look.

◆ *opposite:* A small powder room comes to life with paint and artfully stamped cascading leaves. For the freshest, most current look, a pale background color, such as a tint of yellow, apple green, or lavender, visually expands the small space. Leaves are stamped randomly without measuring or spacing. If too many leaves are stamped and the effect appears crowded, paint out excess leaves before stamping the second coat of paint. A white fabric shade, white mirror frame and shelf, and stacked white towels finish in clean spa-style. Accessories are limited to white cups and a forsythia-filled glass.

◆ **DIAMONDS,** *opposite,* update time-worn, less-than-pristine walls with an engaging new finish. Rather than mask imperfections of aged plaster, the decorator simply measured, taped, and painted over the wall with the sophisticated diamond motif. Colors mimic the natural look of aged plaster. Decorative beads from a crafts store are glued at the points for finishing touches. In a larger room, restrict this much drama to a focal-point wall. **See pages 254–255 for hand-painted diamond technique.**

◆ **PLAID,** *above***,** decorates an upstairs bath in a new suburban house. The homeowner taped and painted horizontal bands for color. For the plaid effect, walls were retaped and rolled with diluted white latex paint.

kitchens

The kitchen—usually one of the busiest and most used rooms in your home—should also be one of the most welcoming and appealing spaces with which to surround yourself.

It is a popular gathering place for family and friends, late-night snacks, and heart-to-heart talks. So, make it a memorable place to share with those who take part in life's moments through the use of decorative painting.

If the kitchen is your decorative painting challenge, why not use a simple sponging or ragging technique in stripes with vibrant colors. Or, for an eat-in kitchen, try a combing technique below the chair rail for some added interest. The amount of wall space and time involved will be small but the impact enormous, and it just might be the inspiration you need to complete another room or two.

Another simple decorative painting method is stenciling. They are easy to use and with a variety to select from, they allow you the freedom to choose patterns and colors that tie in with your own individual style. Use a combination of stencil motifs on walls, furniture, and accessories to freshen up existing spaces that need a little boost, without a lot of expense.

For high traffic areas, choose techniques and paints, such as semigloss latex finishes, that can be wiped clean. Floors in need of attention can benefit from decorative painting with cheerful, creative color combinations and techniques.

Try one or more of the many techniques of decorative painting in your kitchen and enjoy the ambience you can create yourself.

◆ **STRIPES,** *opposite,* in soft neutrals set a stylish but not dominating tone for a kitchen decorated for entertaining and family living. Stripes amplify but don't distract in kitchens and breakfast rooms where the fabrics and collections are in the forefront. When you choose neutral colors, it's easy to achieve a new look or seasonal changes with quick switches of accessories. As a counterpoint to the stripes, unfinished wood cabinets in this kitchen were washed with diluted paint for subtle color that allows the grain of the wood to show. To achieve the effect, dilute latex paint with water and rub on with clean rags. **See pages 242–243 for stripes technique.**

bold & bright

FRESHEN UP YOUR KITCHEN BY PAINTING A BUILT-IN TO SERVE AS THE CONTRAST TO PAINTED FURNITURE PIECES. Use crisp white to lighten and brighten small rooms or rooms with little natural light. Choose a pretty wall color that works with the colors of your painted pieces. When you can't narrow your color choices to one or two, embrace diversity by painting chairs in a medley of your favorite lively shades. Paint one chair style in three or four compatible colors, or choose chairs that combine styles and detailing.

◆ *opposite:* Three different tinted stains transform inexpensive chairs into an upbeat personal design statement. The opaque stains enrich with color while allowing subtle hints of wood grains to show through. A rugged farm table with a protective glass top is an appropriate companion to the rainbow hues of chairs. **See page 295 for techniques.**

◆ *top right:* Shapely chairs, purchased unfinished, recall the country styles of 19th-century France, Italy, and Sweden— and contribute a stylish touch to the dining room. The built-in cabinet has been updated with white paint, after sanding and priming, to cover the original dark, heavy stain. It makes its new appearance as a handy storage piece and room divider in a comfortable family cottage.

◆ *below right:* Vibrant color turns a basic, unpainted dining chair into a striking design statement. Raw wood soaks up yellow stain for deep color; a second coat and matte varnish guarantee long wear and durability.

TOGETHER, COLOR AND PAINT ARE THE NATURAL QUICK-CHANGE ARTISTS. INSTANTLY, A FRESH COAT OF PAINT REVIVES A TIRED OR DATED INTERIOR AND UPDATES STYLE. If you find a room too dark or closed in, change its personality with white, off-white, or the palest tint of a pastel. Light colors give a room a clean, new feel. And, light shades are famous for visually expanding small rooms. For an airy effect, paint woodwork and built-ins the same pale shade or a complementary light tint. Contrast between light and dark painted or stained wall finishes will chop up a room so it feels smaller. Dark stained paneling can be painted. If your drywall is in good condition, choose paint with some sheen to reflect light. Eggshell and satin finishes are options. If you like more shine and light reflection and an easy-to-clean surface, try a semigloss finish.

freshen up

◆ *opposite:* White paint instantly refreshes a once-dark-paneled casual dining area. Note the hanging cupboard and even the wide mat for the watercolor are white. For interest, vary textures when one pale dominates. Here, the cupboard has been distressed with a light sanding for a stylish, casual country accent.

◆ *right:* Paint a furniture piece bright white and experiment with fun accents. To keep it simple, choose such motifs as the pastel stripes, the freehand checkerboard trim, and the polka dots. Use enamels or seal latex paint with polyurethane. Add pulls, in fun shapes, to update the look.

COLOROPTIONS *Add touches of pretty colors to white schemes for freshness. Medium blues, greens, yellows, or pinks are good choices.*

COLOROPTIONS

◆ **STUCCO FINISH,** *opposite,* enlivens a small, budget-conscious, dine-in kitchen with buckskin color and texture that warm the crisp black and white scheme. The finish, done with a specially formulated textured paint, works particularly well as the shelving stands out against visible wall space.

◆ **STUCCO FINISH,** *above,* creates the backdrop for the combination of utilitarian and decorative elements. Repeat the wall color in several accessories, such as picture mats and bowls, to tie such an edited scheme together.

◆ *above:* The simplicity of this dining room is enhanced by the soft palette of colors chosen. Painted in a buttery yellow tone, the chair rail and window trim brings out the painted details in the chairs surrounding the table. A warm hue of green gives authenticity to the distressed side table and corner cabinet which accents the room and gives it a country American appeal.

◆ **CHECKERBOARD FLOOR,** *opposite,* animates a country kitchen of neutral colors and vintage furnishings. The fun comes from the 24-inch-square scale and the contrast with the narrow-striped walls. The taupe repeats for the window trim. **See pages 238–241 for checkerboard technique.**

◆ **HAND-PAINTED VINES,** *opposite and above,* introduce a playful, more youthful mood into a small breakfast room with inherited furniture. The key to the success of this whimsical look is the oversize, stylized character of the hand-painted, curvy vines and white flowers. The edited palette of yellow, green, and white, based on the family's china, glassware, and collected pottery, works effectively with the lighthearted look.

As a further unifying element, the vine's shade of yellow-green repeats for the base of the built-in and for the window trim. **See pages 258–259 for technique.** The wall behind the shelves contributes to the scheme as decoratively painted faux tiles, similar to a faux-tile technique on **pages 250–251.** To continue the visual interest, the floor is a crisp black-and-white checkerboard tile.

◆ **STIPPLING,** *below,* bridges the design trends of vintage and high tech for kitchen remodelings. In this older home with a modern, commercial-grade kitchen, decorative walls repeat the deep colors of the restored home while introducing a note of texture and blending colors. Colors amplify the adjoining room and work with the copper range hood and granite countertops. Stippling is done as part of the leather technique. **See pages 262–263 for stippling (leather) technique.**

◆ **STIPPLING,** *right,* in sun-drenched shades of gold recalls Italy and the South of France. The colors and technique meld for the inviting backdrop the owners wanted for a dining area furnished with a natural-fiber, outdoor-style woven table and chairs. The gold tones also contrast beautifully with the purple glass insets, as they are opposites on the color wheel. Select warm, rich shades of blending colors when your goal is to energize a room. Simple furnishings stand out against such backgrounds. **See pages 262–263 for stippling (leather) technique.**

◆ **CHECKERBOARD,** *left,* illustrates the color options for painted floors. Here, rather than opt for the classic black and white, the owners selected sage green and cream as an anchor for a kitchen and breakfast room designed around pink willowware and floral fabrics. The floor's pattern appears visually quieter than diamonds. **See pages 238–241 for checkerboard technique.**

◆ *below:* The rustic appearance of this kitchen cabinet is brought more into view when placed next to the painted, aged green paneling inthe stairway.

◆ **GLAZED FADED FRESCO VARIATION,** *opposite,* adds style to a budget remodeling, with a wall finish that gives character to a remodeled kitchen. As with faded fresco, the paint is brushed on in wide, loose, random strokes. However, for sheen, a finish coat of clear glaze was applied to the wall. **See pages 248–249 for faded fresco technique, and pages 270–271 for the smoked stain technique.** As a further economy move and style update, stock cabinets were stripped of glaze and color-washed with diluted latex paint. The repetition of the faded shades of green, from glazed walls to washed cabinets, upgrades the look of vinyl tile flooring and an economical laminate countertop. Black and white acts as a crisp, tailored accent. Keep in mind kitchens are ideal rooms for such improvements as they are typically seen as key selling points when a house is on the market.

◆ **CHECKERBOARD ON DIAGONAL,** *above,* updates a country kitchen short on storage and long on charm. In keeping with the scale of the open room and wainscoting, diamonds are 18 inches square on the diagonal. Noticeable grooves between the boards are part of the natural appeal of the distressed and aged look, which the owners emphasize with stools as plant stands. **See pages 238–241 for checkerboard technique.**

◆ *left and below:* A collection of blue and white pottery and porcelain determines the color scheme for a cozy breakfast area where sturdy, unfinished chairs are painted four shades of blue enamel. The table, an unfinished piece chosen for its gently curving legs and apron, sports a sponged top and a simple edging detail. The four shades of blue aptly illustrate that you can create a one-of-a-kind look with paint and basic techniques. For an extra decorative accent, a stenciled fleur-de-lis motif graces the back of each chair; a stylized flower or a motif selected from the blue and white pottery would work equally well. Floral and striped fabrics adorn seat cushions and pillows. **See page 303 for techniques.**

REFINE CABINETS WITH PAINT TECHNIQUES THAT CONVERT FREESTANDING OR BUILT-IN UNITS INTO STYLISH FURNITURE. For such pieces to serve as low-key backdrops for collections, paint them to match other woodwork in the room. To make them focal points within the room, give pieces subtle, yet interesting, paint finishes or embellish the trim.

◆ *right:* A new paint job for this desk with built-in storage above transforms a once-dark corner into a chic home office and study nook. Departing from the standard, a finish painted to emulate linen fabric graces the unit. The chair keeps its original stained finish but is updated with plaid and floral fabric in complementary colors. **See page 303 for techniques.**

◆ *below:* Delicate hand-painted details and faceted glass pulls provide the attention that turns standard painted furniture into memorable accent pieces.

◆ *below:* Crackling is a popular finish that "ages" new pieces, allowing the base to show through small irregular cracks. Crackling is an appropriate background finish for collectibles.

◆ *left:* An easily accomplished crackling technique adds the charm of antique furniture to an unfinished cupboard placed in a combination breakfast room and kitchen. The ivory-over-oak scheme serves as the perfect contrast for a collection of 19th-century brown and cream transferware. Painting the base color to complement a collection further enhances that collection. A collector of blue and white transferware, for example, might choose a clear medium blue base coat. As alternatives, only the inside of the unit could be crackled, the inside could be painted a contrasting shade, or only the sides and drawers could be crackled. **See page 288 for techniques.**

special places, inside & out

To create an inviting, pleasing-to-the-eye environment, rely on the simple use of decorative painting.

Whether inside or out, decorative painting will revitalize walls, floors, stairs, and furniture and enrich those beloved places in your home. Choose colors and patterns that will complement your collections, displays, and interests.

Enliven flea market finds, or spruce up family hand-me-downs to brighten and lighten an area. Mix and match the old with new and freshly painted pieces of furniture.

The use of painted furniture pieces, walls, and floors can add a touch of whimsy, or simply tie a room together for a one-of-a-kind atmosphere. Create an entire room or just a favorite spot around painted furniture or add a few small accents, such as stenciled tables for an outdoor porch or a painted cabinet to embrace a special collection in an entryway.

Add bright accents of red or yellow, and you'll have lively schemes that adapt to a variety of styles and decorating moods.

To warm up a room, turn to appealing soft yellows, heated up by vibrant reds. Or, when drama is your goal, consider the enduring power of red or the sophistication of jewel tones to create special places inside or out, with instant presence. With so many choices to consider, the possibilities are endless.

Mix found treasures with painted furniture for inviting fresh-air living and dining spaces.

outside & in

ENJOY WARM-WEATHER RELAXATION IN A SCREENED PORCH WITH COMFORTABLE SEATING, PILLOWS AND THROWS, TABLES FOR DRINKS AND SNACKS, AND COMPLEMENTARY ART AND ACCESSORIES. Envision the porch as a comfortable retreat that makes the most of valuable space. Shop at secondhand and vintage furniture stores for painted and distressed furniture that add charm and age to the setting. Pair old or distressed pieces with new reproduction painted furniture or with unfinished pieces that you decide to paint. Highlight old pieces by cleaning them and touching them up as needed, letting their age define them. Use well-made vintage or secondhand furniture that can be repainted to suit your scheme or palette. In this most relaxed of all living and dining areas, introduce a medley of fragments and collections that you most enjoy.

◆ *right:* The timeless color combination of green and white reflects summertime freshness, as illustrated by this generously sized screened porch. An assortment of mismatched furniture, along with personal treasures, provides charming appeal. The settee's crisply tailored plaid seat cushion defines order and balance in the eclectic room. The gently worn finish of the vintage twig chair is a rustic accent for garden appeal. The green mid-20th-century-style wicker chair is enhanced with a coordinating floral pillow. The tongue-and-groove cabinet lends a rustic quality and provides always-needed storage.

RUMMAGING THROUGH YOUR ATTIC, A SECONDHAND STORE, OR AN ANTIQUES SHOP MAY UNCOVER THE PERFECT PAINTABLE FURNITURE TO ACCENT YOUR INFORMAL LIVING AND DINING SPACES. You may need only to clean pieces that will become welcome additions into your home. Brush dirty pieces lightly, then scrub gently with mild soap and water. If young children will use or play around the pieces, prevent contact with lead paint by brushing off all loose or chipping paint. Use polyurethane to seal the furniture.

◆ *above left:* A worktable with a drawer adds storage and charm while doubling as a lamp table. Space under the leggy table is put to use to store functional and decorative boxes.

◆ *opposite, top right:* A painted accent chair adds stylish charm to the decor. Small, practical pieces can be used in many settings—porches, bedrooms, entry halls, and dining areas. Accent chairs of differing styles can be painted in similar colors to mix and match, creating a coordinated look within the room. Use decorative chairs in place of small tables to hold books, frames, plants, and other aesthetic items.

◆ *opposite, bottom:* Painted chairs relax a dining room while comfortably pairing with a natural wood table. The contrasting blue sideboard is indicative of the color and charm of the American country and colonial styles of painted furniture. Accessories such as metalware and quilts, shown in cool shades of blue and green, create a restful palette, allowing cow paintings to become a design statement. Barn red and buttery yellow are also typical country colors.

◆ *above:* Assembled from porch columns and architectural trim, the pale green country-style étagère furnishes whimsy on a large scale within a living and dining area full of eclectic furnishings and collectibles. The soft green echoes the floral-print fabric covering the mid-20th-century upholstered armchair. This one-of-a-kind painted piece, definitely a find for a collector who needs display space, neatly organizes an array of boxes and painted tole accessories.

CHOOSE A FABRIC YOU LOVE AS THE INSPIRATION FOR A PERSONAL DECORATING SPACE. Look for a pattern with both the colors for the background walls and furniture and the motifs to translate into stencils. Graphic, stylized motifs are ideal because stenciled details can be simplified. Depending on your time and skill, base one or several stencils on the fabric.

◆ *opposite:* The youthful floral print works perfectly as the design inspiration for a living room decorated in the garden cottage style. The fabric's grid design repeats in a larger scale for the painted wall, created with masking tape and two colors of paint. Five motifs are pulled from the fabric to create the stencils, with designs randomly stenciled. Purchased unfinished, a painted armoire anchors a corner and displays plants settled in baskets. Accent pillows in compatible fabrics finish the look in style.

◆ *above:* The white background allows stenciled flowers in botanical motifs to appear as though they are framed. Subtle shading and delicate green leaves combine as naturalistic interpretation without the necessity of detailed overlays.

SEARCH FOR PAINTABLE FURNITURE THAT HAS DECORATING POTENTIAL AT FLEA MARKETS, SECONDHAND STORES, AND ANTIQUES SHOPS. Select pieces that are in scale, proportion, and are of appropriate style for the room and furnishings into which you plan to incorporate them. Examine pieces for sturdiness and reasonably good condition, allowing for minor repairs. For furniture that you plan to paint, determine whether the surfaces are paintable, whether obvious damage can be repaired, and whether the repairs merit the cost and the work involved. For previously painted furniture, you may only need to sand rough spots and prime before repainting in your color choice.

◆ *above:* A promising find from a vintage furniture store, the Swedish-style daybed is updated with a cushion, bolster, and pillows to enhance a living room. Such worthwhile investments fit into a variety of settings.

◆ *opposite:* Aging and distressing techniques produce a cupboard that reflects a refined rustic setting. Reproduction pulls furnish an authentic touch, and color-washed walls provide a contrast for the distinctive furniture.

cozy corners

FROM THE CLASSIC 18TH-CENTURY CHINESE EXPORT PORCELAINS TO THE PRETTY FRENCH COTTON SCENIC TOILES TO CRISP AWNING STRIPES, NO COLOR COMBINATION IS MORE BELOVED THAN BLUE AND WHITE. Though clear medium and deeper blues are often paired with tints of whites and off-whites, the shades of blue are as endless as the sky. From the intensity of midnight and cobalt blue to the delicacy of the palest, coolest tint, you can find the perfect shade or shades of this always-favorite color. For fun, mix several shades of blue or different patterns, such as combinations of toiles, checks, stripes, prints, plaids, and florals. To avoid visual overload, choose only one dominant print or floral and let the other patterns be supporting players. Mix in porcelain and pottery pieces and you'll have a scheme as easy as it is stylish.

COLOR**OPTIONS**

◆ *opposite:* Tailored, yet lighthearted, stripes translate well into multifunctions, such as this padded window lambrequin and window seat cushion. Notice how the block-print style floral pillow, in the same size as the striped pillow, and the casual combination of blue-and-white accessories bring the scheme to life.

◆ *above:* When you want to keep your scheme on the light side, choose an open print with white background to showcase blue motifs. Restrict your scheme to one cotton or linen print, here a toile style, to keep the look cool and calm.

COLOROPTIONS *From sky to sea to a baby's eyes, blues are everywhere.*

◆ *above:* With a subtly painted screen as a backdrop, this reading nook looks and feels cozy, not spare. The lamp—with fabric shade and distressed base—wicker armchair, and throw add the warmth of texture with minimum color and pattern distraction.

calm & quiet

Think of a room that lulls and soothes, where the background, furnishings, and art together create a peaceful environment. When your goal is quiet, no element should shout for attention. Here, pale furnishings and fabrics impart a traditional feel to a muted background that would have related as well to a contemporary treatment. Varying textures, such as wicker, carved wood, and brass, play against the serene noncolors. To make such a quiet look work, choose shades in discernible variations. In this casual seaside house, the taupe stripes, scenic fabric, and dark wood are the darkest elements, the walls and floors the lightest. The scenic fabric and photographs are still muted, creating interest without disturbing the calm mood.

◆ *above:* Vary the styles, sizes, and finishes of your furniture and lamps when colors are subtle. Dark wood pieces, carefully chosen for shape and detail, add weight to a light palette.

COLOROPTIONS *Soft shades of stone gray and taupe create an alternative to beige and eggshell white. Instead of yellow, add gentle color with shades of delicate, sunrise mauve.*

START WITH BLACK AND WHITE AND YOU'LL DEVELOP A SCHEME THAT'S AS VERSATILE AS IT IS TASTEFUL AND EVER STYLISH. Strong in its own right, the neutral noncolor scheme gracefully accepts a vivid third element. When you want a strong statement, add color for walls as the foyer illustrates. Or, keep the scheme easily changeable with smaller shots of pure color. Be sure to choose a hue bold enough to partner with this graphic pair.

make an entrance

◆ *left:* Perfect for this traditional entry hall or a more contemporary setting, the deep burgundy red enlivens the classic black-and-white tile floor and crisp white woodwork. Touches of brass and gilded framing add sparkle to the setting. Variations of red are natural with black and white, as the hot hue warms what can be a cool scheme. **COLOROPTIONS** *Balance the strong graphic quality of black and white with a clear, intense color.*

COLOROPTIONS

Beautifully detailed stenciled motifs enrich an entry hall for a gracious welcome and preview of the stylish rooms that follow.

CREATE AN INVITING FIRST IMPRESSION BY CHOOSING STENCIL MOTIFS THAT ENRICH YOUR ENTRY HALL. Select patterns and colors that enhance architectural elements and set the stage for your decorating scheme.

◆ *left:* Stenciling takes a turn to the formal and opulent for the entry of a grand Tudor-style home. Inspired by the paneled mahogany wainscoting and arched door, the stenciled borders recall the tapestries and rich colors of period houses. The lower border echoes the paneled door and adds a hint of fresh green. The border continues, with squared corners, above the wainscoting and cased openings. Walls lighten the look and are mellowed with glaze to avoid harsh contrast.

When your goal is to add design interest, consider geometric stenciled motifs as alternatives to more complex designs. Such patterns, often used to repeat, detail plain spaces without taking charge of the decor. You'll be able to find all the classic geometric motifs in commercial stencils. Because the lines and patterns are uncomplicated, you may want to try your hand at making custom stencils. These projects feature both commercial stock stencils and a custom design pattern. Whichever fits your project, select color shades with enough contrast to create interest.

◆ *opposite:* Echoing the lines of the cast-iron railing, this stylized pattern details risers in a stair hall. The black accents over the natural oak strengthen the Spanish Colonial ambience of the setting. A tile floor and a tropical palm, potted in a glazed planter, enhance the look. The repetition of black, rather than introducing bright color, unifies the setting and lends a sophisticated note to the decor.

◆ *above left:* Stenciled motifs, based on a quilt pattern, add the perfect country accent to winding cottage stairs. The gently worn steps, cleaned but not repainted for the project, are the perfect foil for the blocks. Yellow accents repeat the mellow shade of the walls, with touches of green to highlight.

◆ *above right:* Interlocking squares, in pale green and light taupe, add appealing design interest to a painted porch floor. The light green painted border emulates a rug and defines the dark green floor. **See page 295 for technique and page 314 for pattern.**

a quick study

Liven up your library, home office, or den with a handsome decorative finish you custom design to fit your style, skills, and room space.

◆ **STREAKY SQUARES,** *opposite,* lend a note of sophistication and low-key texture to a study with a library feel. The oversize squares, which allude to cut and stacked stones, introduce an element of design interest without overwhelming framed art. The tailored look pairs handsomely with the mix of classic and contemporary furnishings often used in home offices.

◆ **RAGGING,** *above,* refreshes a small home office with the instant impact of color and texture. To avoid closing in a tight space, rag loosely in lighter colors and minimize contrast between values. Repeat the color in furnishings, such as this chair, to unify your scheme. In a room with a low, sloped ceiling, rag the ceiling for a flow of color that will make the room feel more open. **See pages 35, 102, and 107 for variations of ragging.**

◆ **PAINTED DIAMONDS,** *opposite,* embellish a den by repeating, in paint, the tones of the wainscoting and trim. The attention to color strengthens the tailored appeal and avoids the distraction of a competing color. The lattice-like effect comes from the overlapping, darker paint. **See pages 254–255 for similar technique.**

◆ **PAINTED DIAMONDS,** *above,* balance the carefully edited, two-color scheme of dark blue and brown with white. The plaid upholstery fabric introduces an additional pattern for interest and warmth. The paint treatment serves as a canvas for the nautical art and memorabilia. **See pages 254–255 for similar technique.**

WHATEVER YOUR DECORATING STYLE, INVITE THE OUT-DOORS INSIDE WITH CHARMING PROJECTS BASED ON STENCILED MOTIFS. Turn an empty corner or a back-door work space into a country garden with casual designs, featuring old-fashioned flowers and garden tools. If you prefer a more formal or traditional look, consider the array of topiary and planter motifs reminiscent of chic, well-groomed European gardens. Whichever you choose, start the project with a light backdrop in a fresh paint shade appropriate to the outdoors and the garden.

◆ *left:* Stenciled over pale yellow walls, the topiary pattern creates a gracious welcome for the entry of an older home. The light yellow energizes and visually expands the small space while creating a feeling of spring even on cold, wet days. The variety of topiary shapes, stenciled in vertical stripes, along with the period glass sconce with hanging crystals, add interest to the setting.

◆ *above:* A commercial stencil with overlays creates the illusion of a watering can casually planted with wildflowers. Tools, both stenciled and real, enhance the background for this hardworking potting area.

◆ *opposite:* A garden lover's back entry, once a drab mudroom, is updated into a cheerful potting shed with the combination of carefully chosen stencil motifs and the necessary pots and tools. As a start, stenciled wildflowers, chosen for scale and elongated shapes, dress up plain cabinet doors. The watering can and flowers stenciled below the cabinet strengthen the scene. For a decorative display, a salvaged bracket suspends a hanging basket—taking advantage of a sunny window location. Shelves neatly organize pots and tools for potting, and a rustic bench adds additional storage. An old wire egg basket as container and a planter for seed packets are appropriate garden-style finishing touches.

porches with pizzazz

CONSIDER A PLAIN CONCRETE PORCH AS A BLANK CANVAS FOR YOUR CREATIVITY. With paint, stencils, and easy free-hand techniques, you can translate a basic setting into a welcoming outdoor area that invites family and friends to enjoy a fresh-air living room.

◆ *opposite:* Lively colors and stenciled motifs transform a plain suburban porch into a well-decorated fresh-air living area. A hand-painted and stenciled "floorcloth" design is actually painted as part of the brightly detailed porch floor, while the ceiling is traditional soft sky blue. Stenciled and hand-painted pillows and terra-cotta pots contribute to the upbeat ambience.

◆ *above:* Stylized stamped flowers, detailed with a metallic pen, turn plain cotton fabric into stylish accent pillows.

◆ *above left:* Decorated with stenciled stars on a green background, the floorcloth features a decorative banded border, courtesy of stamping and hand painting. Overscaled stenciled flowers and leaves prove the power of paint and bright colors.

See page 306 for technique and page 317 for stencil patterns.

EXPERIENCE THE POWER OF PAINT WITH PORCH PROJECTS THAT TRANSFORM THE STANDARD INTO THE SPECTACULAR. For the most vibrant appeal and setting, paint the porch floor as well as a floorcloth. If you use the porch during the summer exclusively, add a small painted area rug for a finished, decorated look. Adapt color-block techniques by taping off and painting solid color blocks and diamond shapes. Include touches of black for sophisticated accents. Stencil commercial motifs that coordinate with your style, or craft your own stencils from room design elements. For an even simpler process, decoupage or stamp painted furniture and accent pieces with stylized floral or geometric designs.

◆ *above:* A combination of painting and stenciling embellishes a serviceable bench and a pair of ladder-back chairs in this entryway porch. Dramatic black and olive green anchor lively and fashionable violet and yellow accents in the bench seat. The trend of mixing patterns is evident in the diamond pattern and stenciled cherries motif. **See page 309 for techniques.**

◆ *top right:* The stenciled panels, framed by a painted border, recall botanical prints. A floral-print pillow and an architectural fragment complete the stylishly casual scene.

◆ *right:* Design interest is added with a diamond harlequin pattern on the seat that allows the color and design of the stenciled cherry motif to stand out on the back of the bench.

furniture with style

PUT A FRESH NEW FACE AND LIGHTHEARTED SPIN ON THE CLASSIC
PORCH ROCKER WITH A MIX OF FOUR PRETTY PASTELS. Any porch
rocking chair with slats will do for this project—including
previously painted or stained chairs that are in sturdy and
paintable condition. For added interest, look for chairs with
ornate finials or other trim details that can be singled out for
contrasting paint colors.

◆ *below:* On sunny, warm days these lively, painted rocking chairs
migrate from the covered porch to the garden deck for neighborly
conversation. The color scheme for each chair is based on one of the
four pastels. **See page 308 for techniques.**

◆ *right:* Bands of trim are applied with a small artist's brush to detail the
finials. The mix of color blocks and differing details from chair to chair

contributes to the sense of festive, relaxing summertime fun.

◆ *above:* Paint and pattern, in a vibrant palette, unify three unmatched outdoor chairs and a cast-off table base into a patio-cafe-style setting. Hand painting transforms chairs into art, while taping off yields precise lines to the stylized tabletop. **See pages 310–311 for techniques.** A floorcloth, taped off and painted by the same artist, defines the setting with vibrant color block diamonds and the fluid movement of waves.

◆ *left:* The artist lightly pencils the sun-and-moon face on both sides of the painted folding chair before painting the project. As one alternative, the moon face could be drawn and painted before the diamonds are filled in. Another alternative could be to paint the diamonds and then freehand-paint or stencil the moon, sun, or other motif over the

◆ *left:* Accessories such as the rustic birdhouse perched on the column impart personality to a porch setting. **See page 307 for techniques.**

◆ *below:* Stock trim purchased from a home center details a stock porch swing. The unfinished porch swing is assembled, detailed with the trim, and sprayed with white paint for an easy interpretation of a classic Victorian-era swing. A light scrubbing provides the aged appearance. For a rustic look, the swing can be assembled without the trim, sprayed a dark green or barn red, and given a worn look with a light sandpapering. A previously painted wicker chair is refreshed with dark green paint to match the table base. **See page 311 for techniques.**

IF YOU ASSOCIATE CLASSIC ADIRONDACK CHAIRS WITH PLEASURABLY IDLE AND LONG SUMMER AFTERNOONS, ENJOY THESE CLASSICS EVEN MORE IN A CREATIVE COMBINATION OF COLORS AND CLEVER DETAILING.

◆ *lower right:* What could be simpler than using two colors of green—a pleasing medium and a yellow-green—to update these classic chairs and footrest? Shades of green in numerous variations from nature's own palette are always appealing in outdoor settings. For a pleasing effect, these greens contrast for definition but are within the same general intensity (brightness) to prevent one green from overpowering another. In a seaside environment, two shades of blue would be as effective. Clear medium blue, plus navy blue; or red, combined with a bright white would set a crisp nautical theme. **See page 308 for techniques.**

◆ *above:* Two deep greens, an olive and a clear medium, create color harmony with the plants and the terrace in a traditional formal garden. To reflect and capture the garden formality, the dark greens resonate the calm of the classic stonework and aged fragments in the handsome setting. Casual motifs and primary colors could look out of place in a garden where Old-World style prevails.

Express your creativity with stenciling and stamping. The basic techniques for both are easy to learn and offer economical home decorating ideas and solutions. With stenciling and stamping, **projects range from simple to elaborate**—with many variations between. The array of products, from precut stencils to paints to brushes, **create beautiful, personal effects.** Once you learn the basic techniques, consider projects with overlays (more than one layer of stenciled designs). Or, try your hand at designing and cutting your own stencil or making your own stamp. As the first step, decide on your motif and gather your supplies. **The projects in this book are based on custom designs created for featured projects** or on easily obtainable commercial stencils. **Patterns are on pages 312–317.** Directions with supply lists are included in this chapter. **Note that stencil projects are based on single-layer and multiple-layer stencils.** Stamping projects are based on stock and custom-made stamps with specific instructions for each. **For this book, projects are created using acrylics, oil-based stencil paints, and latex wall paints.** Acrylic paints offer the advantage of a range of colors that can be mixed for custom colors. Because they dry quickly, they can be mixed with a commercial extender to prolong the drying time. Each featured project here includes a list of recommended paints and colors with the appropriate brushes and other tools.

For most projects, use a stencil brush, which produces shaded effects. The two basic brushes are soft, domed brushes and stiff, flat-topped brushes. Domed brushes are designed for a swirling or stippling (pouncing the end of the brush) motion. This style of brush works well for most stenciling projects. **Flat-topped brushes are designed just for stippling.** Both styles of brushes come in a variety of sizes from 3/8-inch to 1-inch. You may use a larger brush for overall effect and a smaller one for shading. Use **a separate brush for each color. Practice and surface preparation are crucial to a successful project.** For every project, paint a piece of poster board with your background color, then try the stencil. Adjust the color if necessary. For the actual project, make sure the surface—walls, floors, and furniture—is in good condition. Before you start stenciling, plan the placement of the design. Assemble all the tools and materials. **Measure the surface and lightly mark pinpoint positions that line up with the edge of the stencil.** Attach the stencil, with low-tack masking tape or repositionable spray adhesive, at the first point to be decorated. To use spray adhesive, place the stencil on newspaper with the side to be painted face down. Hold the can about 8 to 12 inches away from the surface and spray a mist to cover the entire stencil back. Use a solvent to remove the excess adhesive if necessary. **Put a small amount of paint onto your palette.** If you are using oil cream paint, remove the skin from the paint and **swirl your brush directly in the paint jar.** If using stencil crayons, rub some crayon on your palette, then swirl your brush in it. Work the paint into the bristles. Swirl the paint on the brush onto a clean part of the palette. Wipe off the excess on scrap paper. Too

much paint causes bleeding under the stencil and gives a heavy-looking finish. **Apply paint with a circular or stippling motion** in extremely thin layers, using an almost-dry brush. A cloudy, translucent appearance is the desired effect.

To build up color, apply more layers of paint, allowing drying time between layers. To shade a design, use darker tones for areas in shade and white or a paler shade of the original color for highlights. When the design is completed, remove the stencil. If you missed an area or need extra shading, carefully replace the stencil and touch up as needed.

If you use a stencil with overlays (multiple design sheets), always start with Stencil A and work in alphabetical order. Note that registration lines show where to place the stencils. **Work with one stencil at a time for an entire room or wall.** After the first sheet is stenciled, line up the registration outlines and apply the next overlay (Stencil B). Continue in this orderly fashion. Immediately after finishing, clean brushes used for water-based paint by rinsing under warm, running water. Stencil brush cleaner works well for most stencil paints, even oil-based ones. Towel-dry brushes. To immediately reuse a brush, **finish drying with a hair dryer.** To store, bind a strip of paper towel around the bristles to hold them straight and secure with a rubber band. Let the brushes dry in a warm place and store flat. Also clean stencils immediately after use. If water-based paint has dried, soak the stencil in warm water. Lay the stencil on a flat surface and rub with a damp nylon abrasive pad. Rinse. Clean off oil-based paint with the recommended solvent immediately after use. **Remove spray adhesive** with the solvent recommended. Dry the cleaned stencil with absorbent paper towels, then store flat.

decorative
painting techniques

blended spots

A

B

SKILL LEVEL

Beginner

TIME (NOT INCLUDING PAINTING BASE COAT OR SEALING)

1 day

SUPPLIES

- Blue painter's tape
- Semigloss paint for base coat paint
- Standard roller frame and cover
- Paint tray and liner
- Small artist's brush
- Paint palette
- 1 small tube black acrylic paint (from an art supply store)
- 1 small tube burnt umber acrylic paint (from an art supply store)
- 4-inch, tapered, soft- bristle brush
- Fine-mist atomizer
- Water-based polyurethane

LETTERED PHOTOS MATCH DIRECTIONAL STEPS

- **Tape off moldings, trim, and ceiling.** Paint walls with semigloss background color. (White was used here.) Allow walls to dry.

A **Apply a small amount of black and burnt umber acrylic paint to the palette.** Using the artist's brush, randomly dab small spots of black and burnt umber on the wall. Work in small sections about 2 feet square.

B **Dampen the 4-inch brush with water** and in light sweeping motions, wipe across the paint spots to soften and blend against the background color. If paint spots dry too fast, moisten the wall with water from a fine mist spray atomizer. Continue this process across the wall, working one area into another.

- **To make this washable,** finish by coating the dry walls with a clear coat of glaze or water-based polyurethane.

HELPFUL HINT

- **The technique works best on smooth walls.**

chambray technique

SKILL LEVEL
Advanced

TIME (NOT INCLUDING PAINTING BASE COAT)
2 days

SUPPLIES
- Measuring tape
- Pencil or chalk line
- Level
- Blue painter's tape
- Drop cloth
- Paint for base coat
- Semigloss or gloss paint
- Standard paint roller frame
- 2 lint-free, ¼-inch nap roller covers
- 2-inch trim brush
- Paint tray and liner
- Acrylic aging glaze
- Plastic container
- Edging tool
- 6-inch technique brush for chambray
- Rags
- Masking tape

LETTERED PHOTOS MATCH DIRECTIONAL STEPS

■ **Tape off moldings, trim, and ceiling.** Paint walls with base coat (white was used here) and allow to dry. For best results with this technique, purchase the appropriate kit with instructional video and tools from a home center or specialty paint store. This is a two-person technique. However, for a consistent look, one partner should do all the weave painting. The other is the helper. The idea of chambray is to recreate the look of fabric panels with paint. Because glaze dries quickly, it's best for panel widths not to exceed easy arm's reach from standing or from a ladder, no wider than about 42 inches. It's also important to carefully measure your room so that you can calculate the widths of the panels. If you need to alter section widths to fit the space, place these sections at the corners. For example, depending on the size and shape of your room, it may not be possible for every panel to be exactly your chosen 36 inches wide. In that case, make adjustments at the room's corners.

■ **Use a pencil or chalk to mark sections at the top of the walls**. Use a chalk line to mark your lines. Wipe off the chalk after taping just outside the lines with blue painter's tape.

■ **Mix 4 parts glaze to 1 part paint in a plastic container.** Soak the roller in the glaze mixture and roll it over the tray so it doesn't drip. Roll a thin layer of translucent glaze within your taped panel. Roll as close to the ceiling and trim as possible. Even out roller marks by rolling from ceiling to floor. The glaze will appear uneven and translucent.

A **Dip the edging tool into the glaze.** With a pouncing motion, dab to corners in hard-to-reach areas, especially around trim and moldings. Apply just one layer.

B **Begin at the top of your panel and drag** the 6-inch brush from one side to the other. Reverse the motion on top of the first stroke. Then repeat these two strokes for four horizontal drags; continue down the panel in this manner. Wipe the brush with a rag to remove excess glaze as needed.

C **Begin at the ceiling and brush lightly** downward with one stroke. Don't bend the bristles. Repeat so each vertical line has been covered twice, leaving horizontal brush marks still visible. Remove tape while glaze is still wet. Allow to dry overnight before taping and painting alternate sections.

D **Run masking tape down the dried glaze** about ⅛ inch from the edge so only a very small area will be glazed twice. Complete the unglazed sections, using the same technique as the previously glazed panels.

HELPFUL HINTS

■ **Light pastel shades**, which emulate open-weave fabrics, are attractive in this finish.

■ **You must use the proper 6-inch weaver brush** for the desired effect.

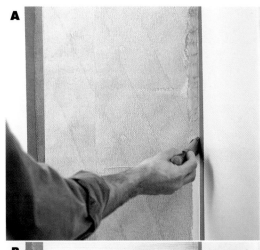

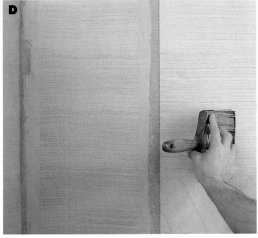

checkerboard floor technique

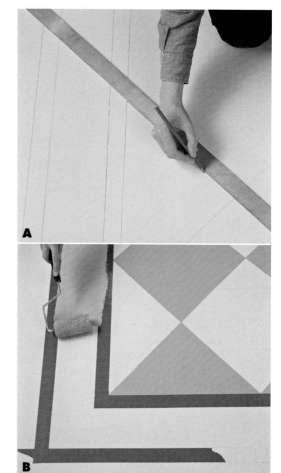

A

B

SKILL LEVEL
Advanced

TIME (NOT INCLUDING PAINTING BASE COAT)
1 to 1½ days

SUPPLIES
- Latex wood filler
- Pad sander with 80-grit sandpaper
- Damp mop
- Primer
- Standard roller frame and cover
- Paint tray and liner
- Tape measure
- Ruler
- Yardsticks
- Graph paper and pencil
- Chalk line
- T-square or right triangle
- Masking tape
- Two paint colors (porch paint recommended for durability)
- 4-inch roller cover and frame
- Paint trays and liners
- Small touch-up brushes
- Polyurethane

LETTERED PHOTOS MATCH DIRECTIONAL STEPS

- **Prepare your floor by filling cracks with latex wood filler**, sanding, and damp-mopping to remove sanding dust. The surface should be clean and smooth. Seal your surface with an appropriate primer if it isn't already sealed and follow directions on the can of porch paint.

- **Decide on the placement of your checkerboard floor design** and whether a border will be included. Any size of "area rug" can be painted onto a wood or concrete floor, or the floor can be filled as in the example, *opposite*. The checkerboard could also be placed on a diagonal.

- **If you are putting the checkerboard design** in the middle of a room or at an angle, decide on the size of the rug. If you are adding the border, lay out the basic rectangle that will be the outside border. For best results, carefully measure your floor area. Then design your checkerboard pattern on graph paper so you know exactly what measurements to use. Or, if you are including a border, you can lay out the border on all sides, then measure and divide the remaining space to find the size of the checkerboard.

- **Make two points to establish one side of the rectangle.** Connect the lines with a yardstick. If working with a partner, which is helpful, you can snap a chalk line. Or use two or three yardsticks taped together to make a long straightedge if you are working alone.

- **Use a right triangle or a T-square** to square the edges for the next side of the rectangle.

- **Extend your yardstick(s) or chalk line** to line up with the right angle you made with the T-square or right triangle. Mark your line with the chalk or pencil.

- **Repeat this procedure for the third side**, then connect the edges for the fourth side. Tape off this rectangle and paint it your lightest color.
- **Measure from the outside edge** of the rectangle to the inside to create the borders. Draw in the borders, using the ruler for measuring, the right angle for 90-degree angles, and the yardsticks for a straight edge. See diagram #1, *below*.
- **The diamond checkerboard pattern** is based on a grid. Measure the shorter side inside the borders and divide by three or more, depending on how many diamonds you want to go across your checkerboard pattern. Measure and divide the long side by five or more, again depending on your space and taste.

▲ **Mark all of the measurements** into the inside border. Connect the marks diagonally to make the checkerboard design. Or mark the other points of the diamond checkerboard pattern, by using the measurements you figured out on graph paper. This technique is easier if you have to work alone. You can connect all of your marks diagonally, sliding your straightedge as you go. See diagram #2, *opposite*.

1

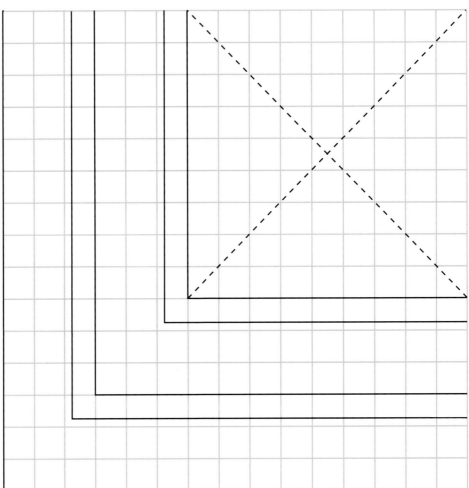

1 SQUARE = 2 INCHES

B After your design is in place, start painting the diamonds. Put a light "X" on each diamond that you want to be painted the darker color. Of the diamonds to be painted, tape off every other one. Keep the drawn lines just inside the tape so they'll be painted over. Roll the paint on with a 4-inch roller, being careful not to roll outside the tape. Re-coat if necessary.

■ **Remove the tape**. Allow the first diamonds to dry thoroughly before you tape off and paint the remaining diamonds.

■ **Tape off the borders in the same way**. Touch up with a small artist's brush if necessary. Allow the floor to thoroughly dry. For durability, seal with two coats of satin polyurethane, allowing drying time between coats.

2

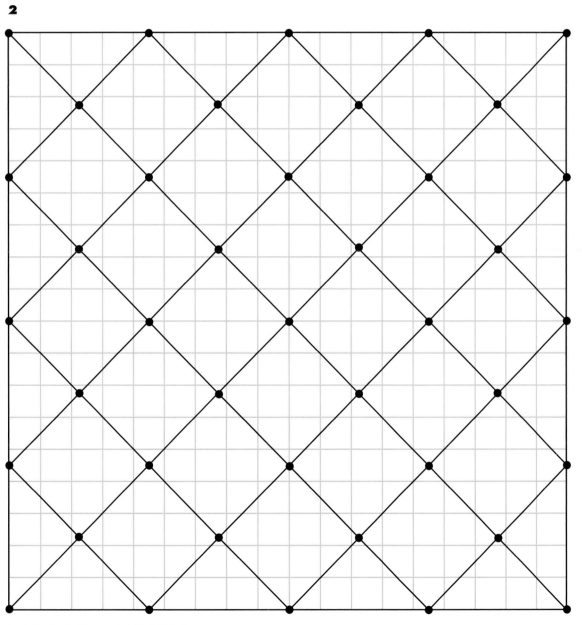

1 SQUARE = 4 INCHES

colorwash & taped stripe technique

SKILL LEVEL

Beginner

TIME (NOT INCLUDING PAINTING BASE COAT)

1 day

SUPPLIES

- Blue painter's tape
- Drop cloth
- Paint for base coat
- Standard roller frame and cover
- 2-inch trim brush
- Paint tray and liner
- Brown paper painter's tape in desired width
- Pencil
- Level
- Paint for stripes
- Latex glaze
- Plastic container
- 3- to 4-inch paintbrush

LETTERED PHOTOS MATCH DIRECTIONAL STEPS

- **The purpose of taped stripes is to simplify measuring.** The glaze, which is brushed on, contributes hand-painted charm. You'll use the width of two pieces of tape, as shown, as the spacing between your stripes. The width of your brush is the width of your stripes.
- **Tape off moldings, trim, and ceiling with blue painter's tape.** Paint wall with base coat paint. Allow to dry.

A Tape the spaces between stripes; this will be the unpainted part of the wall. Using the brown paper painter's tape, tape two pieces together down the wall. Next, use two smaller pieces of the same tape for spacing. Repeat two pieces of tape, running down the wall as shown. Repeat this pattern across the wall. Fudge measurements slightly at corners to compensate for spacing. If you are concerned that taped lines are straight, first create a guideline with a pencil and level.

B Mix 1 part latex glaze, 1 part paint, and 1 part water in a plastic container. Adjust proportions if the mixture seems too thick or too thin. Remove the pieces of spacer tape. Using a brush slightly narrower than the stripes, drag down the glaze mixture from the ceiling. Continue across wall until completed.

C Remove the tape while the glaze mixture is still damp.

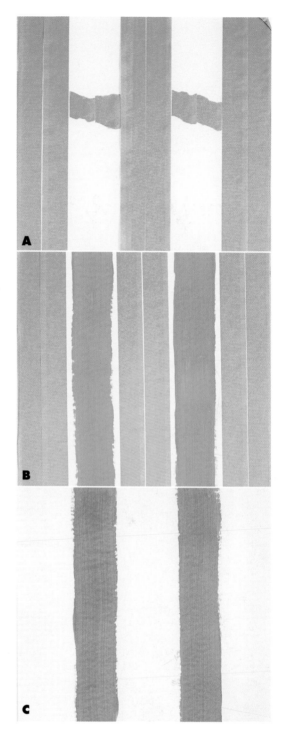

combing technique

SKILL LEVEL

Intermediate
(Complexity comes
from keeping lines
uniform.)

TIME (NOT INCLUDING PAINTING BASE COAT)

2 days

SUPPLIES

- Blue painter's tape
- Drop cloth
- Satin, semigloss, or gloss paint for base coat
- Standard roller frame and cover
- 2-inch trim brush
- Paint tray and liner
- 4-inch roller frame and cover
- Paint for top coat
- Rubber comb
- Rags
- Small artist's brush

LETTERED PHOTO MATCHES DIRECTIONAL STEP

- **Tape off moldings, trim, and ceiling.** Choose coordinating colors with enough contrast to differentiate between the base and the combed top coat. (The base coat here is a grayed medium green, combed with a cream.) Paint the wall with a base coat. Allow the wall to dry thoroughly. Use a 4-inch roller to apply top coat paint vertically to wall. Roll twice for approximately an 8-inch width.

A Holding the comb with both hands, apply even pressure and drag the comb down the wall in one continuous motion. Repeat the process, alternating between rolling and combing. Wipe the comb as needed with a damp rag.

HELPFUL HINTS

- **This technique works well on smooth walls.**
- **If you are using a multisided rubber comb,** you may need to cut off one or two sides to allow the comb to reach into corners.
- **If the comb feels too flexible as you work,** tape it to a putty knife.
- **When you are using paint without glaze** as in this example, work only in small areas to avoid paint becoming unworkable. The addition of glaze will lengthen the drying time, but the technique is still most easily done in narrow sections.
- **When working from an inside corner to an outside corner,** begin at the inside. As you comb across the wall, you don't have to worry about the placement of the comb when you approach the outside corner.
- **When combing into an area narrower than the comb,** use a small artist's brush and paint back slightly into the area already combed to widen the final width of paint to accommodate the width of the comb.
- **Comb adjacent walls on different days,** or if done in the same day, allow at least four hours between walls to avoid smudging.
- **Vary the look of basic combing** by combing zigzags, cross-hatching, or swirls. You don't have to comb in a straight line.
- **This technique is fairly easy but requires a steady hand.** Corners can be tricky.

double-roll technique

SKILL LEVEL

Beginner

TIME (NOT INCLUDING PAINTING BASE COAT)

1 afternoon for 1 wall

SUPPLIES

- Blue painter's tape
- Drop cloth
- Two coordinating colors of latex interior paint
- Double roller kit should include:
  - Double paint tray
  - Edging brush
  - Double roller
  - Decorative roller covers
  - Edging and accent sponges

LETTERED PHOTOS MATCH DIRECTIONAL STEPS

- **Tape off moldings, trim, and ceiling.** Start with painted walls in good condition. This is your background color. Practice the following technique on a board to find the look you like. Pour paints into the divided paint tray. Don't mix paints. Dip a small "pouncing" or edging brush into both colors of paint. Using a dabbing motion, dab the paint into the corners and around the top edge of the wall. Starting at the top, paint only a small section of the edges and corners. It works best to do a two-foot section of edges and corners so they blend well into each other.

A&B Dip double roller into paints. Each side of the roller will be a different paint color. Roll with the double roller, up and down, and back and across until you get an amount of blending you like. Dip the accent sponge into paint and work the edges while they are still wet. It works best to do a wall in sections that you can roll easily.

C Continue rolling, edging, and accenting the wall. Take the time to step back and look at your work. Look for consistency. For variation, apply heavier pressure on one end of the roller and lighter on the other.

D For finishing touches, dip the accent sponge into the paint and press randomly. You can add additional accents, if you think they are necessary, after the wall is dry.

HELPFUL HINT

- **Double rolling is ideal as a focal point wall**, such as around the mantel, or in a small room such as a powder room. Select colors that blend, rather than contrast, for the most pleasing effect.

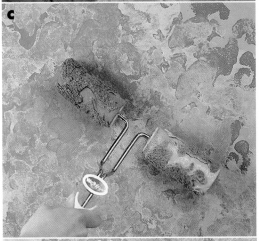

faded fresco technique

LETTERED PHOTOS MATCH DIRECTIONAL STEPS

■ **Tape off moldings, trim, and ceiling.** Paint your walls with a satin-finish base coat. (Light khaki was used here.) Water down flat white paint to a half-and-half mixture in a plastic container.

A **With a 4-inch-wide brush**, brush on the mixture with loose, random strokes. Vary your strokes so the mixture is more opaque in some areas, much lighter in others. Continue to brush out drips or runs, feathering the paint with your brush to avoid hard edges. Before the paint is completely dry, blend and wipe away some of the white with a clean, damp rag. Allow the walls to dry thoroughly.

B **Make a color wash** by mixing 4 tablespoons of burnt sienna into ½ gallon of water. Brush on liberally. As it dries, lightly brush runs to avoid drips. Be sure to cover the entire wall. (The paint will appear heavier in some areas.)

C **After the walls are dry**, repeat the color wash, using 4 tablespoons of yellow oxide to ½ gallon of water. Apply in the same manner as the previous color wash.

HELPFUL HINTS

■ **This is a very messy technique.** Applying color washes is like painting a giant watercolor on the wall. Be sure to have an ample supply of drop cloths and clean rags.

■ **When mixing the paint and water**, begin by adding a few tablespoons of water to the paint and mixing thoroughly. Add water slowly and continue to mix. If paint, especially acrylic paint, is added to a large amount of water all at once, it won't disperse. When mixing acrylic paints and water this way, stir the mix frequently to avoid pigments settling to the bottom. This mix cannot be stored because the pigments settle out.

■ **Step back from the wall** several times during each step and look to see where you might want to add or subtract a little color.

■ **Be sure to work out to the edges** of each wall, carefully getting paint into corners and all the way to the ceiling and down to the baseboards. This gives more unity to the walls.

■ **Note that the finish will be fairly flat** and not suitable for high-traffic areas. Attempting to wash it will remove pigment from walls. However, it can be clear-coated, but this affects the surface sheen. The technique works well on both smooth and textured walls.

SKILL LEVEL
Intermediate

TIME (NOT INCLUDING PAINTING BASE COAT)
1 day

SUPPLIES
■ Blue painter's tape
■ Drop cloth
■ Satin paint for base coat
■ Standard roller frame and cover
■ 2-inch trim brush
■ Paint tray and liner
■ Flat white wall paint
■ Three plastic containers
■ 4-inch paintbrush
■ Tablespoon
■ Water
■ 4-ounce tube burnt sienna acrylic paint (from an art supply store)
■ 4-ounce tube yellow oxide acrylic paint
■ Lint-free rags

A

B

C

FADED FRESCO VARIATION
(PICTURED ON PAGES 32–33)

Follow the directions for faded fresco. However, instead of brushing on white, rag on white in two even layers over the entire painted wall (over red-based terra-cotta on pages 32–33). Allow to dry. Make two washes—from watered-down sienna and from watered-down yellow oxide acrylic. Brush on the sienna, then the oxide wash. (Artist acrylic paints are sold at art supply and crafts stores.)

faux-tile floor technique

FAUX-TILE FLOOR
SKILL LEVEL
Intermediate

TIME (NOT INCLUDING
PAINTING BASE COAT)
1 day

SUPPLIES
- Blue painter's tape
- Graph paper and pencil
- Latex primer or porch paint
- Standard roller frame and cover
- 2-inch trim brush
- Paint trays and liners
- Colored pencil
- Straightedge
- 1- or 2-inch flat artist's brushes
- Three coordinating colors of latex paint
- Lint-free rags
- No. 7 artist's brush
- Two colors of crafts paint
- Polyurethane

LETTERED PHOTOS MATCH DIRECTIONAL STEPS

- **Tape off baseboard molding.** This pattern was created by drawing a grid of squares in a diagonal pattern across the floor. For best results, use graph paper to draw to scale the perimeter of the floor and the grid pattern so you can see how the pattern lays on the floor. Prime the floor with latex primer following manufacturer's instructions.

A **Using a colored pencil and a straightedge,** very lightly draw a straight line from one corner of a square to the opposite corner, bisecting the square and leaving it divided into two triangles. Continue these lines across the floor so half the squares are bisected and half of the squares are whole.

B **With a 1- to 2-inch flat artist's brush,** loosely fill in the squares with your choice of latex or porch paint. Leave about ⅜-inch of white around the perimeter of each square. Fill in the triangles with two other latex colors, in the same loose manner, again leaving some white around the perimeter of each.

C **Use a damp rag** to wipe off pencil lines.

D **With a No. 7 rounded artist's brush,** paint freehand circles with crafts paint at the intersections where six points of squares and triangles meet. With the same brush and the second color of crafts paint, paint dashed lines through all of the white areas that surround the squares and triangles.

- **Seal with two coats** of water-based, satin-finish polyurethane, allowing adequate drying time between the coats.

FAUX-TILE WALL

- **Start with a light, clean wall**; paint off-white if necessary.

- **If the wall is freshly painted,** allow it to dry thoroughly. Using a straightedge, level, white paint, and small brush, freehand paint the mortar lines that will divide 4×4-inch tiles. Freehand painting will keep the effect loose and casual. For easy spacing, start at the center of each wall and work out.

- **Using a small roller for each color,** paint inside mortar lines. While the paint is wet, brush over each tile; use separate brushes for each color.

- **Allow the painted wall to dry thoroughly.** Thin leftover off-white paint with acrylic urethane and brush over the walls for a color-washed effect.

FAUX-TILE WALL

SKILL LEVEL

Intermediate

TIME (NOT INCLUDING PAINTING BASE COAT)

1 day

SUPPLIES

- Blue painter's tape
- Drop cloth
- Eggshell finish, off-white latex paint
- Standard roller frame and cover
- 2-inch trim brush
- Paint trays and liners
- Straightedge and level
- Eggshell finish, white latex paint (quart)
- Small paintbrushes
- Two 4-inch roller frames and covers
- Two shades of latex paint in your choice of colors
- Acrylic urethane
- 3- to 4-inch paintbrush

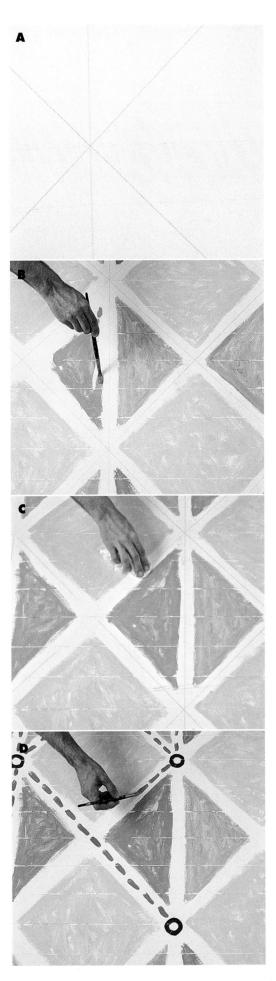

flower border technique

SKILL LEVEL

Beginner

TIME (NOT INCLUDING PAINTING BASE COAT)

½ to 1 day

SUPPLIES

- Level with printed ruler
- Colored pencil
- Drop cloth
- Three colors of latex paint
- Small paintbrush
- Artist's brushes

LETTERED PHOTOS MATCH DIRECTIONAL STEPS

- **The fun of this border is its lighthearted,** stylized look. Choose bright, clear colors for an appealing effect.

A Measure with level and colored pencil in two horizontal lines at the desired height. Here, the lines are 8 inches apart. Measure and lightly mark center points every 9 inches.

B With a small brush and the border paint color, draw an outline of the daisy around every other spot. Draw a small circle around the other spots.

C Paint the border with your color choice.

D Use the artist's brushes and paint the flowers' center in the second color and the spots in the border with a third color.

HELPFUL HINTS

- **Standard chair rail** height is 32 to 34 inches.
- **Note the pencil lines,** which are marked heavily to be visible for instruction. For your home projects, mark as lightly as possible to avoid dark lines showing through.

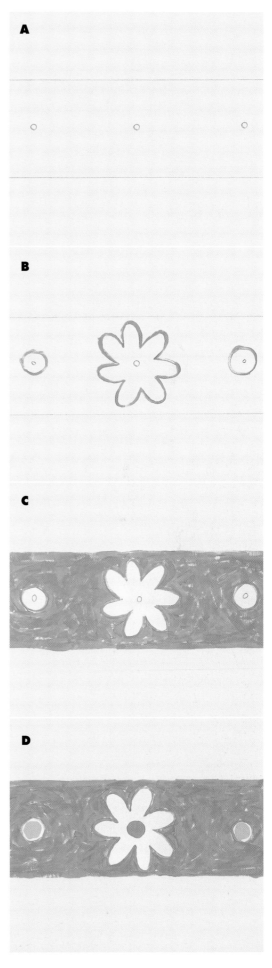

hand-painted diamond pattern

SKILL LEVEL
Intermediate

TIME (NOT INCLUDING
PAINTING BASE COAT)
1½ to 2 days

SUPPLIES
- Level with printed ruler
- Cork-backed ruler
- Colored pencil and
sharpener
- Drop cloth
- Paint in your choice
of three colors
- Medium or large
round, tapered
artist's brush
- Quarter-size coin
- Small round, tapered
artist's brush

every other mark will be 18 inches. You'll see a pattern emerging. When you finish measuring and marking, diagonally connect the lines with a colored pencil and ruler, and draw your grid.

A **To paint the diagonal grid**, use a medium or large round, tapered artist's brush dipped in your paint. Hand paint over the diagonal lines of the grid, starting at the top of one diagonal and moving all the way down to the bottom, dipping your brush as needed. Do all the diagonals in one direction first. If a second coat of paint is needed, simply dip your brush and trace over your lines again. Allow these lines to dry before you paint the other diagonals in the same manner.

B **After all of your lines are dry**, trace a quarter at each intersection. Using the smaller brush, paint in the circle.

C **After the circles are dry**, paint a ring around each circle with another color of paint, again using the small round artist's brush.

HELPFUL HINTS

■ **If you want a thicker or thinner line for the grid**, adjust your brush size accordingly. Adjust the size of the circle with a silver dollar or other circular object.

■ **Remember, the lines don't have to be perfectly straight**. The purpose of the hand-painted pattern is to add some interest and variety in line widths.

LETTERED PHOTOS MATCH DIRECTIONAL STEPS

■ **Choose the scale and placement** of the diamond pattern. In this project, the diamond is 18 inches in height and 15 inches in width. Finding the points of the diamond is the key to laying out the diamond grid.

■ **Begin by measuring and marking pencil dots** on the wall. Start at the corner where walls meet the ceiling and measure half of the width of your diamond design. Here, the full diamond width is 15 inches, so the measurement across is 7½ inches. Measure every 7½ inches across until you reach the end of the wall. Use your own measurements to best fit your space.

■ **After the horizontal measurements are in place**, measure down half the height of your diamond—here 9 inches. From the 9-inch mark, measure down 18 inches, then down another 18 inches, etc., until you reach the bottom of the wall.

■ **Return to the top of the wall** and locate your first half-width mark. Measure down from there to 18 inches, again using your level, and every 18 inches until you reach the bottom. Continue measuring down the wall in this manner. Remember that the first mark down will be 9 inches from every other mark at the top of the wall. And

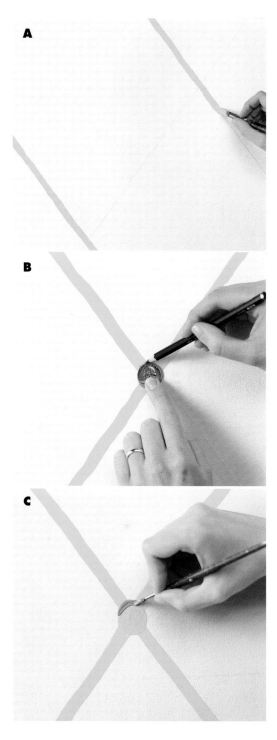

A

B

C

hand-painted vertical stripes

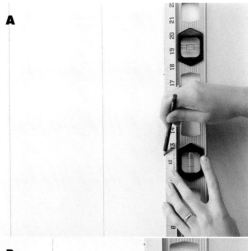

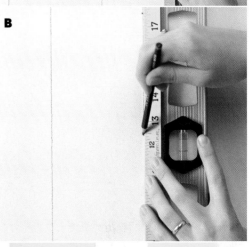

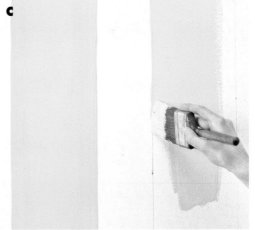

SKILL LEVEL

Beginner

TIME (NOT INCLUDING PAINTING BASE COAT)

1 day

SUPPLIES

- Blue painter's tape
- Drop cloth
- Paint for base coat
- Standard roller frame and cover
- 2-inch trim brush
- Paint tray and liner
- Level with printed ruler
- Colored pencil
- Paint for stripes
- 2- or 3-inch paintbrush

LETTERED PHOTOS MATCH DIRECTIONAL STEPS

- **Tape off moldings, trim, and ceiling.** Choose your colors and widths. The colors may contrast or be differing values of the same color. Paint your walls in the base coat color. Allow to dry.
- **Start at the top of the wall** and make a series of measurement marks moving horizontally across the top. In this project, the stripes are 6 inches wide with 4 inches between each. If you want to avoid a stripe around a corner, it's acceptable to fudge your measurements a bit. Or you can allow the stripe to fold around the corner, depending on your preference.

A & B When the measurements are completed, use a level to draw lines from ceiling to floor. Draw lines lightly and use a colored pencil if possible. Protect the moldings and trim with painter's masking tape.

C For a charming, hand-painted look, simply paint the stripes on the wall, starting at the edges and filling in. It works best to start at the top and paint in about 12-inch sections. If necessary, apply a second coat after the first is thoroughly dry. Carefully remove painter's tape while paint is still wet.

hand-painted vine pattern

SKILL LEVEL
Beginner

TIME (NOT INCLUDING PAINTING BASE COAT)
1 day

SUPPLIES
- Blue painter's tape
- Drop cloth
- Paint for base coat
- Standard roller frame and cover
- 2-inch trim brush
- Paint tray and liner
- Measuring tape
- Level with printed ruler
- Pencil
- Green crafts paint for vines and leaves
- Small tapered artist's brushes
- Crafts paint for accent color

LETTERED PHOTOS MATCH DIRECTIONAL STEPS
- **Tape off moldings, trim, and ceiling.** Paint your walls in the base coat color. Allow to dry.
- **Measure your walls.** Determine the number and spacing of the vines you would like.
- **A** **Measure and mark pencil spots** so they line up equal distance both vertically and horizontally.
- **B** **Connect the spots vertically** with alternating curving lines.
- **C** **With green crafts paint and the artist's brush,** paint the vertical lines to resemble vines.
- **D** **Paint leaves using the inside curve** of each vine as a guide. Add round accents in a second color below each leaf, or randomly as shown in *opposite* photograph.

HELPFUL HINTS
- **Use colored pencils if possible.**
- **Choose** a round, tapered No. 10 artist's brush to hand paint vines and leaves.
- **Practice your leaf technique on a board** before you attempt the wall.

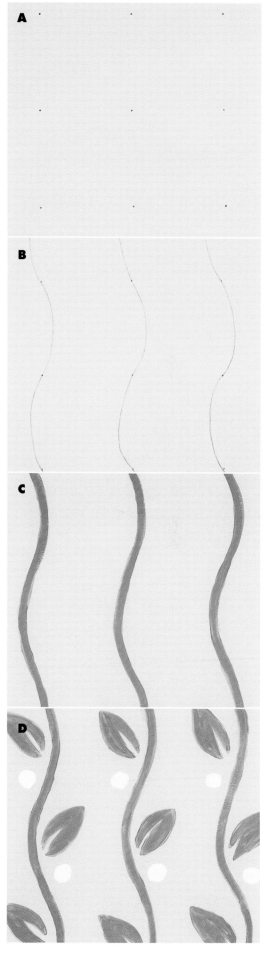

harlequin diamond pattern

SKILL LEVEL
Intermediate

TIME (NOT INCLUDING PAINTING BASE COAT)
1 day

DIAMOND SUPPLIES
- Optional: Latex paint for base coat in desired color and finish
- Latex paint for top coat in desired color(s) and finish
- Painter's tape
- Roller or paintbrush and paint tray
- Colored pencils (to match paints)
- Tape measure
- Lint-free rags
- Yardstick
- Carpenter's level
- Graph paper

1. If desired apply a base coat to the wall in the lightest desired color.

2. Measure the wall to be painted and choose the size and scale of the diamonds. Using graph paper draw out the desired diamond design. (In the diagram shown right, the diamonds are 6 inches tall and 4 inches wide; the following directions are for those dimensions. The large-scale diamonds, *opposite*, are just an enlargement of the same proportions.)

3. Starting at an upper corner of the wall, where it meets the ceiling, measure half of the width of the diamond design (in our example 2 inches) and make a mark with a colored pencil. After that mark, measure the full width of the diamond design (in our example 4 inches) across the wall until you reach the end.

4. Return to the first mark made in Step 3. Measure down from this mark the height of the diamond (in our example 6 inches); make a mark here. Continue across the wall, using the marks made in Step 3 as a guide, until you reach the end.

5. Using the first mark made in Step 4, continue measuring the marking the height of the diamond until the entire wall is marked. The height of each diamond has now been measured.

6. To measure and mark the width of each diamond, return to the first mark made in Step 3. Measure down half of the height of the diamond (in this case 3 inches) and then across half of the width of the diamond(in our example 2 inches).

Make a mark here. After that mark, measure the full width of the diamond design across the wall until you reach the end.

7. Using the first mark made in Step 6, continue measuring and marking the width of the diamond until the entire wall is marked. The width of each diamond has now been measured.

8. When you are done measuring and marking the entire wall, diagonally connect the lines with a colored pencil and yardstick, creating the diamond design.

9. For crisp diamonds, use painter's tape to mask off the lines and tape an "X" within each diamond not to be painted. Paint the diamonds with the top coat paint; remove the tape and let dry.

10. For casual, looser appearance, do not use painter's tape to mask off the diamonds; simply use the colored pencil as a guide and paint the diamonds with the top coat paint.

leather technique

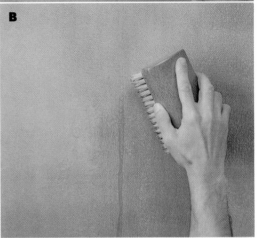

SKILL LEVEL

Advanced

TIME (NOT INCLUDING PAINTING BASE COAT)

2 days

SUPPLIES

- Blue painter's tape
- Drop cloth
- Paint for base coat
- Standard roller frame
- Two paint trays and liners
- 2-inch trim brush
- Paint tray and liner
- Semigloss or gloss paint
- Acrylic aging glaze
- Plastic container
- Edging tool
- Stippling brush
- Lint-free rags

LETTERED PHOTOS MATCH DIRECTIONAL STEPS

- **Tape off moldings, trim, and ceiling.** Paint the walls in your choice of color. The rich colors of old leather furniture, such as browns, camels, aged gold, oxblood red, dark blue, or forest green, work well for this look. (The example here used an aged gold.) Leave tape on and allow the walls to dry overnight.
- **Make sure you have help;** creating leather walls takes two people. As with all techniques, practice first on boards. Mix 4 parts glaze to 1 part paint in a plastic container. Pour the glaze into a paint tray; soak the roller in the glaze for a minute or so. Move the roller back and forth so it doesn't drip. At the corner of the room, roll a single vertical stripe. Roll from the middle of the first section up toward the ceiling; roll down to evenly spread the glaze. Apply only a single strip of glaze.
- **Dip the edging tool into the glaze.** Dab glaze into hard-to-reach areas missed by the roller.
- **A** **Start stippling with your stippling brush** as soon as one strip of glaze has been rolled on. Brush in a quick, pouncing motion, beginning at the top of the wall and working down. Leave at least 2 inches of outer edge of strip not stippled.
- **B** **Roll another roller width of glaze** on the wall adjacent to the first, being careful not to overlap glaze of the first section. Quickly stipple to blend the seam between the two sections. Regularly alter the angle of your wrist when you stipple to avoid creating a pattern.
- **C** **Clean the bristles of your stippling brush** with a rag after every 15 or so pounces. Use the edging tool along the ceiling and molding to blend the stippled areas.

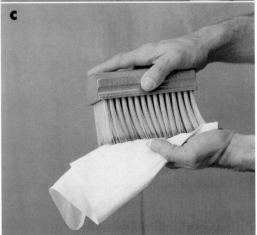

- **Remove the tape from the ceiling** and molding before the glaze is completely dry.

HELPFUL HINTS

- **Be prepared to work fast** as the glaze becomes unworkable in about 15 minutes. This is a fairly involved technique. For more detailed instructions, purchase a kit with an instructional video at a home center or specialty paint store.
- **If you can't complete a room in a day,** stop at a corner. Tape off the corner of the adjacent wall to make sure all the glaze stays on the side of the room you are completing.

moiré stripes technique

LETTERED PHOTOS MATCH DIRECTIONAL STEPS

■ **This technique works best on smooth walls. Tape off moldings, trim, and ceiling.**

■ **Paint the walls in your choice of color.** Use satin paint for the background. (A rich, earthy yellow was used here.) Measure for the placement of 5- to 6-inch stripes, making sure that stripes are several inches away from the door and window moldings and corners of the walls.

■ **Using a level and a colored pencil** similar in color to the paint, draw lines to determine the width of stripes. Tape off floorboards and ceiling. Tape off outside of stripes.

■ **Mix the glaze mixture**. Start with half paint and half glaze. (White paint with a dash of the yellow base coat was mixed with the glaze for the featured project.) Test the mixture on a practice board for the appropriate color and density. (The mixture should roll on easily without dripping.) Adjust paint, color, or glaze as needed to get the look you want. Using a 4-inch roller, apply the glaze mixture to the wall.

A **Immediately, using a comb made from a squeegee**, and starting parallel to and against the ceiling, make a continuous "S" pattern down the length of the stripe. Be sure the comb covers the width of the stripe without going beyond the outer edges of the tape. Wipe paint from the comb with a rag.

B **Begin at the top again**, but this time, make the reverse "S" pattern. This creates the moiré stripes. Carefully remove the tape.

HELPFUL HINTS

C **Make the squeegee comb by cutting out grooves** with a crafts knife.

■ It isn't important that the stripes match perfectly in width. Some can be a little wider and others narrower.

SKILL LEVEL
Advanced

TIME (NOT INCLUDING PAINTING BASE COAT)
Several days
(Measuring and taping are time consuming.)

SUPPLIES
- 2-inch blue painter's tape
- Drop cloth
- Satin paint for base coat color
- Standard roller frame and cover
- 2-inch trim brush
- Paint tray and liner
- Tape measure
- Level or ruler
- Colored pencil
- Latex paint
- Acrylic aging glaze
- Plastic container
- 4-inch roller frame and cover
- Crafts knife
- Comb made from 7-inch squeegee
- Lint-free rags

plaid technique

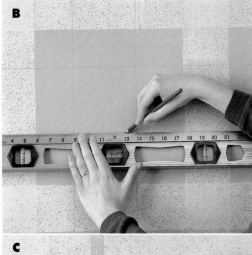

SKILL LEVEL
Advanced

TIME (NOT INCLUDING PAINTING BASE COAT)
2 to 2½ days

SUPPLIES
- Blue painter's tape
- Drop cloth
- Level with printed ruler
- Four colors of satin paint
- Colored pencils to match your paint colors
- Rectangular kitchen sponges
- Paint trays and liners
- Paper bag for blotting
- Lint-free rags
- Sharp scissors

LETTERED PHOTOS MATCH DIRECTIONAL STEPS

- **For the best results**, decide on the colors and scale of your plaid and practice on boards until you perfect a pattern you like. (For this project, tan, green, and light blue paint were used.) Layer your color choices in different combinations and try small, medium, or large kitchen sponges to change your scale. You may like a simpler plaid design with one or two colors and a less complex pattern.

- **To create your pattern**, you'll measure out the largest part of the plaid, which is the background plaid that is sponged on by the whole, flat sponge. The other two plaid colors are sponged on with the sides of the sponge. These thinner bands are applied over the dried thicker plaid. Tape off moldings, trim, and ceiling.

- **Start the plaid in the most prominent area** of the wall. Refer to the graphic pattern for measuring on **page 268**. The sponge used in this example was 3½ inches wide on the broad side and 1 inch wide on the edges. These two measurements from the sponge create the layout.

- **Referring to the graph on page 268**, measure and mark the vertical lines of the largest part of the plaid. Use a level to extend from your mark to make the vertical lines run from the top of the wall to the bottom.

- **Lay in the horizontal lines of the large plaid**. Measure the same distance as before, but horizontally only. Use the level to extend the horizontal lines all the way across your wall. This is the basic structure of your plaid.

- **Wet the sponge and wring it out**. Pour a small amount of paint into the paint tray and gently dip your sponge into the paint, then immediately blot off excess paint on the clean end of the paint tray and/or on a paper bag.

A **Begin sponging the vertical lines.** Keep the sponge to the right of the vertical line and press firmly with the sponge placed vertically on the wall. You will be able to sponge three to four times before you have to dip into the paint. An arrow drawn on the back will help to orient the sponge in the same direction each time.

■ **Continue sponging until all the verticals** are in place. If you have a tight spot where the sponge is too large to fit, wait until you are done with most of the room and cut down the sponge to fit. If the plaid doesn't break evenly at a corner, wait until the end and cut down the sponge to fit.

Sponge horizontal lines by placing the sponge on the underside of penciled-in horizontal lines.

B **After the largest part of the plaid dries**, draw the vertical and horizontal lines for the smaller parts of the plaid, on top of the existing plaid. Refer to the second graph on **page 269** for help with measurements and layout. Sponge in the thin parts of the plaid. Starting and finishing with the second color, before you start the third color.

C **Use the narrow edges of your sponge** and sponge to the right of the penciled lines. Trim down the sponge if necessary to fit into tight spaces. A second or third sponge may be used to trim down if necessary.

1

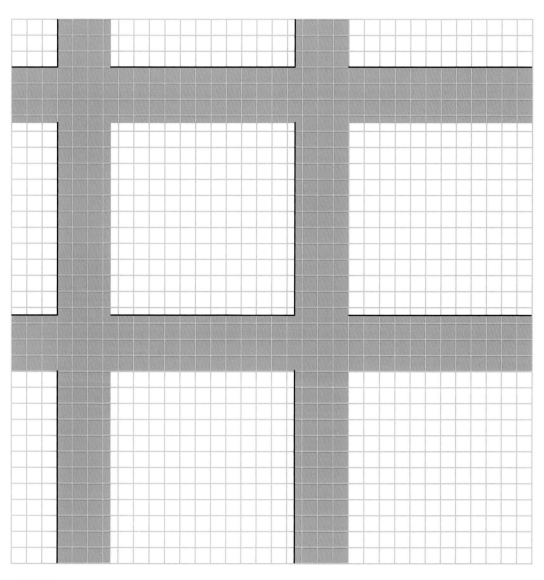

1 SQUARE = 1 INCH

HELPFUL HINTS

- **This is a good technique to repeat** wall colors used in your home.

- **Because the technique is time consuming,** consider it for small rooms or as a focal point.

- **Windowless walls are easiest.**

2

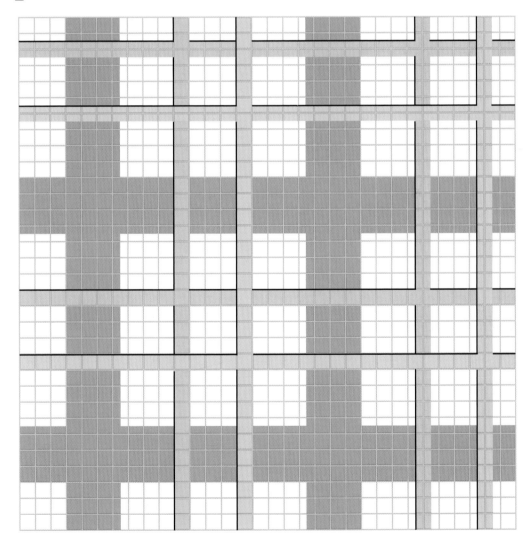

1 SQUARE = 1 INCH

ragging off & smoked stain techniques

SKILL LEVEL
Intermediate

TIME (NOT INCLUDING PAINTING BASE COAT)
2 days

RAGGING OFF/SMOKED STAIN SUPPLIES
- Blue painter's tape
- Drop cloth
- Satin paint for base coat color
- Standard roller frame and cover
- 2-inch trim brush
- Paint tray and liner
- Acrylic artist's paint
- Glaze
- Tablespoon
- Plastic container
- 4-inch trim brush
- Lint-free rags

LETTERED PHOTOS MATCH DIRECTIONAL STEPS
RAGGING OFF

■ **Tape off moldings, trim, and ceiling. Paint the base coat with satin paint**. (A cream color was used here.) Add 4 tablespoons of acrylic artist's color to 1 quart glaze in a plastic container. Stir well to mix. Cut in with the 4-inch trim brush around the ceiling, baseboard, and corners as you go.

A Work in sections of about two roller widths at a time. Roll on two roller widths of glaze.

B With a clean, dry rag, blot the glaze so the rag removes some of the glaze. Continue blotting down the wall, replacing each saturated rag with a fresh one. Do not blot off to the edge of the wet glaze. It's important to roll down the next strip of glaze to the edge of the previously rolled portion of rolled glaze.

■ **Begin ragging the seams to blend** the two sections. Then rag down the wall and continue the process across the wall.

■ **Allow the ragged walls to dry thoroughly.**

SMOKED STAIN

C Mix the glaze as in ragging off.

■ **Use the 4-inch trim brush to apply the glaze along the perimeter** of the walls and around window and door frames. Work in sections as wide as you can stretch your arms. After first applying glaze, make one continuous sweep with the brush as far as you can comfortably reach.

D Continue to lightly brush the glaze, feathering it out so it is darker in the corners and fades to lighter shades. (The idea is to re-create the look of a room aged by smoke.) On long stretches, continue the process along the length of the wall.

■ **Glaze horizontal strokes one day and allow to dry overnight**. The next day, paint vertical strokes, making sure the glaze accumulates around moldings and in corners for the desired effect.

HELPFUL HINTS

■ **This technique works well for smooth or textured walls.**

■ **Commercially available paper rags work well**. They are sold in dispenser boxes and are sturdy and lint-free.

■ **Note that fresh rags pick up more glaze** than saturated ones. Use accordingly as you work so you don't remove too much glaze every time you change rags.

■ **You'll only have about 10 minutes** to remove glaze before it becomes unworkable. Don't go back over a section that is partially dry. The glaze will not blend better.

■ **For larger wall areas, enlist a partner**. One person should roll while the other blots with rags.

■ **As an alternative to mixing your glaze**, use a commercially available one with pre-mixed pigments.

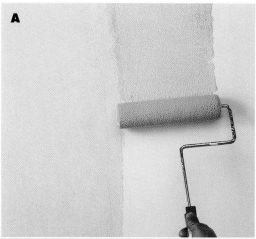

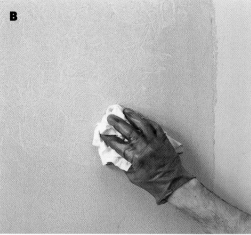

rolling & ragging technique

LETTERED PHOTOS MATCH DIRECTIONAL STEPS

A Tape off moldings, trim, and ceiling. Select **two colors from the same family** that are near one another on a color chart. (Two shades of olive tans are used here.)

B Pour each color into a separate paint tray. Using small rollers, randomly roll each color on the wall.

C Blend some as you go so the wall is covered with variations of the two blended colors. Don't leave any hard lines. Allow the walls to dry thoroughly.

D Choose a third color several shades lighter than the lightest color used. Dilute the color with three parts water to one part paint. Wear gloves for protection. Submerge a cotton rag in diluted paint. Squeeze out paint. With the rag loosely wadded, press it against the wall. Try to have enough paint in the rag so it shows but not so much that it runs when pressing. Continue to turn the rag in your hand, re-gathering it and pressing it against the wall a dozen times or until you decide you need more paint. Continue this process over the entire wall.

■ **After the wall is dry**, rag on another layer of watered-down paint if you think too much of the under-painting is showing through.

HELPFUL HINTS

■ **This technique works well for smooth or textured walls.**

■ **This technique is very messy**; have lots of clean rags and drop cloths on hand.

■ **Half of a clean, cotton T-shirt**, with sleeves, neck, and hem removed, works well for this paint application.

SKILL LEVEL
Intermediate

TIME (NOT INCLUDING PAINTING BASE COAT)
1 day

SUPPLIES
- Blue painter's tape
- Drop cloth
- Three flat paint colors within the same family on the color chart
- Two paint rollers
- Two paint trays and liners
- Plastic container
- Latex or rubber gloves
- Soft cotton rags

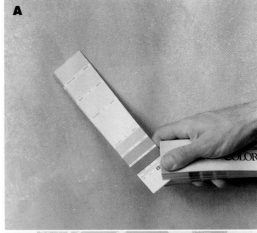

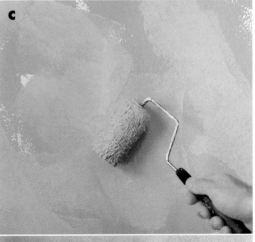

sponging technique

SKILL LEVEL

Beginner

TIME (NOT INCLUDING PAINTING BASE COAT)

½ to 1 day

SUPPLIES

- Blue painter's tape
- Drop cloth
- Paint for base coat color
- Standard roller frame and cover
- 2-inch trim brush
- Paint tray and liner
- Paint for sponging
- Natural sea sponge
- Newspapers for blotting
- Cardboard for corners

LETTERED PHOTOS MATCH DIRECTIONAL STEPS

- **Tape off moldings, trim, and ceiling.** For this project, diluted off-white paint was sponged over pale yellow walls. If you are painting a base coat, allow it to dry overnight.

A Wet your sponge with water, wringing it out thoroughly. Pour a small amount of paint into a tray or pie tin. Dip the sponge into the paint and blot excess on newspaper. Cup the sponge in your hand and push lightly onto the surface.

B Space the patches of color evenly, but change the position of the sponge for an irregular, mottled effect. Close, overlapping marks have a sleek look; widely spaced sponging with little or no overlapping appears more casual. Try spaced first; then fill in.

C Use a piece of cardboard, held up with one hand in a corner, to protect the opposite corner from being over-sponged. Use a small piece of sponge to work in corners.

HELPFUL HINTS

- **For the most pleasing effect**, choose colors without jarring contrast. If you want to add second and third layers, consider choosing your colors from the same paint card for a pleasing, subtle effect.

- **As an alternative**, loosely rag on diluted paint with a lightly gathered, not rolled, cotton cloth. Blend as you rag for a pleasing effect.

streaky squares technique

LETTERED PHOTOS MATCH DIRECTIONAL STEPS

■ **Tape off moldings, trim, and ceiling.** Choose the scale for your room. Measure the walls to determine what dimensions will work. If your measurements won't come out evenly, fudge a bit at the corners of your walls where exact measurements aren't as obvious. Twenty-four-inch squares were chosen for this project. Paint the base coat color. Allow to dry.

■ **Make a grid on your wall by marking off** every 24 inches on your wall. Start at the top corner. Mark every 24 inches across the top of the wall and down the corner to the floor. Extend the marks from the ceiling down to the floor, using a level and pencil. Next, extend the horizontal marks out from the corner in the same manner.

■ **Now you have a simple grid.** Squares should alternate between horizontal and vertical streaks. To keep the horizontal and vertical patterns in the correct order, mark either a horizontal or vertical arrow in each square with your colored pencil.

A **Mask off every other square** in the uppermost horizontal lines of squares. Work one square at a time. Open your three small cans of paint. You need to work quickly within each square. Dip your 2-inch

paintbrush into the lightest color and streak the square. Gradually streak in the medium shade. Be careful not to apply too much paint to avoid drips.

B&C **Add the darkest paint for accents.** Work each square until you achieve the look you want, but do so quickly enough that the paint doesn't dry between steps.

■ **Carefully remove the tape from each finished square.** When you tape off the square between the finished squares, keep in mind that you may allow a little bit of the background color to show through by not butting the tape directly up to the adjacent finished square. The background color showing through provides contrast to the streaks.

■ **Repeat the taping and streaking** until all the squares are completed.

HELPFUL HINT

■ **Choose three colors varying in value and intensity** from a paint chip card. Paint stores often have five to six tones of one color on a paint chip card. Choose a light, medium, and dark accent color. To choose a background color, think of a color that will provide a touch of contrast. For example, the background color here is a cool gray, which contrasts with the warm golden brown tones of the streaky squares. Do not make the background color too bright; only a little contrast is necessary.

strié (dragging) technique

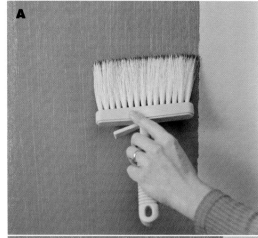

SKILL LEVEL

Intermediate

TIME (NOT INCLUDING PAINTING BASE COAT)

1 day

SUPPLIES

- Blue painter's tape
- Drop cloth
- Satin paint for base coat
- Standard roller frame and cover
- 2-inch trim brush
- Paint trays and liners
- Tinted glaze
- Large, stiff-bristled brush
- Lint-free rags

LETTERED PHOTOS MATCH DIRECTIONAL STEPS

- **This technique requires two people.** Make sure your walls are smooth. Choose a background color that will show through the glaze. Tape off moldings, trim, and ceiling. Paint the base coat color. Allow to dry.

A **The basic technique is rolling glaze** over the painted wall and then removing some of the glaze by dragging a brush with stiff bristles from the top to the bottom of your walls. This allows some of the background color to show through and creates a pleasing visual texture.

B **One partner rolls the tinted glaze in vertical stripes**; the second removes some of the glaze by dragging a dry brush down the wall. Bristles need to be lightly touching the wall for best effect. Maintain a light, steady pressure.

- **Wipe the dragging brush on clean rags** to remove excess glaze.

HELPFUL HINTS

- **One partner should be rolling the second vertical stripe while the other partner is finishing dragging the first**. Stripes should overlap.
- **Both partners should work quickly**; neither can stop in mid-wall. Tape off adjacent walls so glaze doesn't seep around corners.
- **If you find it difficult to drag down in one continuous motion**, stop two-thirds of the way down the wall and drag from the bottom up, feathering your brush up as the lines meet. Stagger the meeting points to avoid the distraction of a horizontal band appearing around the lower portion of your wall.

suede technique

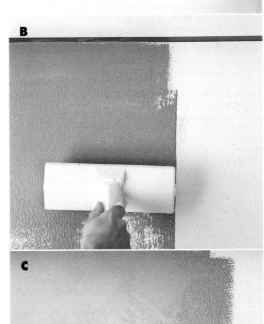

SKILL LEVEL

Advanced

TIME (NOT INCLUDING PAINTING BASE COAT)

2 days

SUPPLIES

- Blue painter's tape
- Drop cloth
- Specially-formulated textured paint
- 4-inch roller frame with foam cover
- Specialized suede roller
- 3-inch brush

LETTERED PHOTOS MATCH DIRECTIONAL STEPS

- **Tape off moldings, trim, and ceiling. Paints to create the textured effects of suede are sold under several brand names.** When you purchase the paint, it's important also to buy the roller covers formulated for your particular brand of textured paint. You'll use about twice as much textured paint to cover a room as you would for standard latex paint. For example, if you have painted a bedroom with one gallon of paint in the past, purchase two gallons of the textured paint. When correctly done, the finish is rich and handsome. However, it is difficult to touch up and is not resistant to moisture. It isn't recommended for kitchens, baths, children's rooms, or other high-traffic family areas. The projects for this book are in an adult sitting room and a master bedroom.

- **Tape off all moldings**, trim, and ceiling.

A **Cut in about two feet** along the ceiling and down the corner of the wall. Use a small sponge roller.

B **Using the suede roller**, apply paint, two roller widths wide, in a vertical motion. Roll over wet paint from ceiling to floor.

C **Brush into the wet paint** with a cross-hatch motion, leaving a couple of inches unbrushed at the edge. Roll several more roller widths and continue to brush across wall in a cross-hatch motion from ceiling to floor. Allow to dry at least four hours.

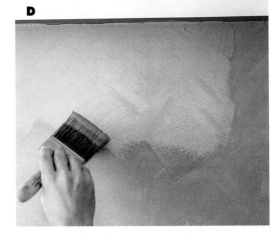

D **After paint has dried**, dip brush in paint. Working quickly in small sections, cross-hatch a second coat of paint on the wall. It is important to work quickly so that you are always working into an edge of wet paint.

HELPFUL HINT

- **One person should do** all cross-hatching so that the brush strokes are consistent.

stencil techniques

GARDEN COTTAGE LIVING ROOM

SKILL LEVEL
Advanced

TIME
3 days

SUPPLIES
- Medium yellow latex wall paint
- Level
- Ruler
- Colored pencil
- Decorators' glaze
- White latex wall paint
- Plastic container
- Acrylic stencil paints
- Tapered brush
- Stencils
- Small stencil brushes

GARDEN COTTAGE LIVING ROOM STENCIL

- **Design and create the backdrop** for stenciled motifs. Paint the wall medium yellow. Allow to dry. Measure and determine the size for the rectangles. (Rectangles shown are 12×16 inches.) Lightly draw in the outlines of the rectangle with a level, ruler, and colored pencil that is similar to the background color.

- **Mix the whitewash** with a ratio of 3 parts glaze to 1 part white paint in a plastic container. Paint with a tapered brush. Design simple stencils with no more than two overlays to each stencil. Choose motifs from a print fabric for a pleasant mix of elements. If you draw, sketch simple shapes. Or photocopy motifs from the fabric and alter the scale on the photocopier to fit the space.

- **Alternately, trace designs** directly from the fabric onto tracing paper, scale up or down with a photocopier and convert into stencils. See page 285 for directions on designing and cutting stencils. For example, design a light green leaf shape with darker green accents. Trace and cut out the stencils. Center the stencil motifs inside every other rectangle.

COTTAGE TULIP WALL
SKILL LEVEL
Advanced
TIME
4 days
SUPPLIES
- Level
- Colored pencil
- Blue painter's tape
- Decorators' glaze
- Pale green and blue latex paint
- Commercial stencil
- Oil-based blue and green stencil paint

COTTAGE TULIP FLOORCLOTH SKILL LEVEL
Intermediate
TIME
4 days
- Floorcloth material
- Scissors
- Primer
- White latex paint
- Green and blue latex paint
- 4-inch roller frame and cover
- No. 10 round artist's brushes
- Commercial stencil
- Medium blue and green stencil paints

GARDEN COTTAGE TULIP WALL STENCIL

- Walls are decoratively painted for a pretty backdrop. Start with white walls, choosing satin or eggshell sheen. With a level and either a light blue or light green colored pencil, draw a series of vertical lines every 10½ inches, starting in a corner and working around the room. Striping two or three walls saves time.
- **Tape to the left** of every line with 2-inch-wide blue painter's tape and smooth down the tape edges. Use a *4-inch mini roller* and roll on a thin layer of neutral (untinted) decorators' glaze to seal the edges of the tape. This prevents the blue and green stripes from bleeding under the tape.
- **After all the tape** is in place, use a *small roller* to paint every other stripe blue; then paint the remaining stripes green. Allow to dry. Carefully remove the tape, revealing the white stripes.
- **Remove the pattern** from the stencil package. Use *scissors* and cut apart the paper stencil image and tape to the wall to determine tulip stencil placement.
- **If stencil comes as a row of tulips,** cut apart for easy maneuvering and use individual tulips.
- **Stencil tulips** around the room, keeping furniture placement in mind. Use medium blue stencil paint for petals; concentrate paint on some edges or add a darker or lighter blue for interest. Use green for leaves; concentrate for shadows. Apply paint with a pouncing motion, using a *medium stencil brush*. Use all three overlays for each tulip.

GARDEN COTTAGE TULIP FLOORCLOTH STENCIL

- **For an easy project, purchase floorcloth material**, rather than canvas. Cut the floorcloth to the size you desire. To cut the oval shape, find and mark the center of each side of the rectangular floorcloth. Draw the oval curve onto one-fourth of the rug.
- **When you are satisfied** with the curve, cut out in one piece. Use this piece as a pattern to trace onto the other three-quarters of the rug. Cut the remaining sides. Draw a scalloped border around the edge and cut with scissors. Place rug on a leak-proof drop cloth. Prime. Using a small roller, paint the entire rug with green latex paint.
- **Allow the base coat** to dry. Recoat if necessary. Paint a blue border onto the rug to mimic the scalloped pattern. With a No. 10 round artist's brush, paint a thin white line that mimics the blue scalloped edge.
- Tape tulip pattern samples to determine placement on the floorcloth. Stencil tulips as directed for the tulip wall stencil. Allow to dry. Seal immediately with a *water-based polyurethane* protector. Apply two to three coats for durability. Coat the back with a *rubber backing* available in an aerosol spray. Allow to dry before placing on the floor.

A

STAMPED LEAF GIRL'S ROOM

SKILL LEVEL

Intermediate

TIME

2 days

SUPPLIES

- 2 computer mouse pads
- Acrylic paint (1 quart each)
  Dark periwinkle
  Dark pink
  Medium pink
  Medium intensity
- Stencil painter roller or similar foam roller
- Lime green latex paint
- 1 quart decorators' glaze
- Plastic container
- 2-inch trim brush

STAMPED LEAF GIRL'S ROOM
(STAMP PATTERNS ON PAGE 312)

- **Choose a fresh, upbeat color scheme.**
Directions are given for the colors featured. You can create your own look based on fabric or accessories. Choose a motif for the stamp. The motif shown is based on the comforter fabric. This project begins with white walls.

- **To make a rubber stamp,** choose a simple design. Draw the motif on paper and cut out. This project features two stamps, measuring 8 inches long and 6 inches long.

A **Trace around the design** onto a mouse pad; cut out with a crafts knife.

B **Roll paint onto the stamp with roller.** Apply the stamp to the wall in a random pattern, leaving room for other stamps. Stamp additional leaf shapes for a visually interesting mix of color.

C **Finish by glazing the walls.** Mix 3 parts glaze to 1 part lime green paint in a plastic container. Use a trim brush and apply the glaze mixture to the wall, leaving white space around each stamp. Cover all other wall areas. Work quickly and avoid leaving hard edges that could dry and resemble lines. If you have to stop, brush out (feather) the lines where you stop. This softens the glaze edges. The amount of glaze/paint mixture needed for a medium-size room is a little more than a quart.

B

C

decorative furniture

AGED PATINA TABLE
SKILL LEVEL
Beginner
TIME
3 days
SUPPLIES
- Eggshell-finish, interior latex paint: white
- 2-inch trim brush
- Crackle glaze
- Two foam brushes
- Antiquing glaze
- Clear, matte-finish spray sealant

ARTISTIC ARMOIRE
SKILL LEVEL
Intermediate
TIME
4 to 5 days
SUPPLIES
- Blue painter's tape
- White and red latex paint
- Antiquing glaze
- Round artist's brush
- Small artist's brush
- Black acrylic paint
- Unused pencil eraser
- Gold leaf paint
- Polyurethane

AGED PATINA TABLE
(PROJECT SHOWN ON PAGE 25)
- **Lightly sand table** with *medium-grit sandpaper*. Wipe with *tack cloth*. Apply white base coat using a 2-inch trim brush and let dry 6 to 8 hours. If original table is dark wood, apply a second coat and let dry.
- **Apply crackle glaze,** following manufacturer's directions, and let dry for 6 to 8 hours. Apply a thin coat of antiquing glaze with a foam brush, allowing the crackle finish to show through. While the antiquing glaze is wet, wipe off excess glaze with a foam brush. Repeat this step to build up layers. Let table dry overnight.
- **Spray the entire piece** with spray sealant. Allow to dry. Repeat. Allow the table to dry for 48 hours before placing objects on it.

ARTISTIC ARMOIRE
(PROJECT SHOWN ON PAGE 26)
- **This project features an unfinished armoire, which was lightly sanded and sealed with primer.** Let dry overnight. Paint white for a dry-brush effect. Let dry 6 to 8 hours. Determine the size and placement of the diamonds, then draw them with a *pencil* and *straightedge*. Tape outside the penciled lines using blue painter's tape.
- **Using the red paint,** dip brush in glaze, then in red paint. Paint the diamonds. Hand-paint the other patterns with a round brush. After the red dries (2 to 4 hours), loosely paint designs over the red paint with a small artist's brush.
- **Add the black dots at the intersections** of the diamonds with an unused pencil eraser dipped in black paint. With a small artist's brush, outline the diamonds with the gold leaf paint. Allow piece to dry completely.
- **Rough up the edges with *sandpaper*** for a worn look; wipe with a tack cloth. Apply two coats of polyurethane; allow drying time between coats.

DINING ROOM TABLE AND CHAIRS
SKILL LEVEL
Beginner
TIME
1 to 2 days
SUPPLIES
- Fine- and medium-grit sandpaper
- Tack cloth
- Latex primer
- 2½-inch trim brush
- Tan paint in eggshell finish
- 1- and 2½-inch-wide gesso brushes
- Nylon scrub pad
- Clear paste wax
- Terry cloth

DINING ROOM TABLE AND CHAIRS
(PROJECT SHOWN ON PAGE 124)

- **This project updates a vintage oak** dining table. The technique also could be applied to an unfinished table. Sand the table with fine- and then medium-grit sandpaper. Remove sanding dust with a tack cloth. Prime the table and allow the primer to dry.

- **Apply a base coat** of tan paint. On top of the base coat, apply a light even coat of primer with a 2½-inch-wide gesso brush, imitating wood grain with your brush strokes. Dry for 1 hour. Dampen a nylon scrub pad with water, and buff away areas of the off-white to reveal the undercoat. Allow to dry. Apply three coats of clear paste wax. Allow drying time after each coat.

- **For a more durable surface,** apply water-based polyurethane in place of wax.

- **The chair project uses unfinished chairs** that have a tight wood grain. Open-grain wood provides a different effect. (Try the technique on the bottom of the chair to determine whether you like the effect.) This technique is not suitable for previously painted chairs.

- **Apply a light coat of primer** with a 1-inch-wide gesso brush. Follow the grain of the wood to prevent brush strokes from showing. As soon as the primer dries, use water-dampened terry cloth to buff away portions of the primer to reveal the wood. Allow to dry thoroughly and apply two coats of clear paste wax.

SWEDISH CUPBOARD
(PROJECT SHOWN ON PAGE 197)
SKILL LEVEL
Beginner
TIME
2 to 3 days
SUPPLIES
- Sandpaper
- Tack cloth
- Gray and ivory latex paint
- 2½-inch trim brush
- Crackle medium
- Polyurethane

- **This project uses an unfinished cupboard. Practice first on a board.** Lightly sand the cupboard; remove dust with a tack cloth. Brush on the base coat over raw wood with the trim brush. Allow to dry.

- **Apply crackle medium,** following manufacturer's directions. Lightly brush on top coat of paint. Do not brush over or attempt to touch up the top coat. Doing so interferes with the crackling. Seal with polyurethane.

FOLK ART MONOGRAM HEADBOARD
SKILL LEVEL

Intermediate

TIME

2 days

SUPPLIES

- Wood glue
- Grass green and cream satin latex paint
- Green colored pencil
- ⅜-inch artist's brush
- Antiquing glaze tinted in gray
- 2-inch trim brush
- Foam paintbrush
- Clear, matte-finish sealant

FOLK ART MONOGRAM HEADBOARD
(PROJECT SHOWN ON PAGE 147)

- **This project is created with a custom-made, unfinished headboard** and stock finials, which are attached with wood glue. Apply one coat of grass green paint and allow to dry. Apply second coat and allow to dry.
- **To place the monogram,** measure the horizontal and vertical center of the headboard. Mark the intersecting spot with a colored pencil.
- **Using this center point as a guideline,** draw the large monogram freehand. Note how the center point falls in the middle of the center letter. Pencil small initials on each side. Finish the design with freehand scrolls.
- **Using a ⅜-inch artist's brush,** paint the monogram cream. Let dry for 6 hours. Apply antiquing glaze with a 2-inch trim brush in quick, broad strokes across the headboard. Immediately rub off the glaze with a clean foam paintbrush, using the same broad strokes.

- **When the entire headboard** has been painted with the glaze-and-wipe technique, repeat the glazing process twice more. Paint and glaze the top and sides of the headboard.
- **After you achieve the desired aging,** let the headboard dry. Seal with clear matte sealant.
- **As an alternative,** stencil the monogram with commercial stencils, varying the sizes for interest. If you find a lettering style you like, enlarge it on a photocopier to make a stencil. Follow the stenciling directions on page 285. Another variation is to decoupage your motif, following the decoupage directions on page 296.

FRENCH BLUE AND WHITE SIDEBOARD CHEST

SKILL LEVEL
Intermediate

TIME
2 days

SUPPLIES
- Blue and white flat latex paint
- 2-inch brush
- Dark brown furniture wax

MOROCCAN TABLE

SKILL LEVEL
Advanced

TIME
4 to 5 days

SUPPLIES
- Red latex paint
- Two 2-inch paintbrushes
- Red pencil
- Small artist's brush
- Crimson, amber, aqua, blue, white, black, burnt umber acrylic paint
- Watercolor brush
- Crackle glaze
- Water-based, satin-finish polyurethane

FRENCH BLUE AND WHITE SIDEBOARD CHEST
(PROJECT SHOWN ON PAGE 125)

- **This project uses a vintage sideboard.** Remove existing hardware. Lightly sand the entire piece with *medium-grit sandpaper*. Wipe with a damp rag or *tack cloth*. Apply two coats of *primer* with a 2-inch brush. Determine the size of the motifs by measuring the chest. Work out the pattern for your design on *paper*. Pencil in guidelines and then sketch the design freehand onto the chest.
- **Using the picture as a guide,** paint the chest, using blue and white paints. Let the paint dry. With white paint, dry-brush (use a brush with only the tips dipped into the paint) over the areas painted blue. Allow to dry overnight.
- **Sand the entire chest** with *fine sandpaper* for a worn and distressed look. Sand edges to expose the dark wood underneath. Wipe with tack cloth.
- **Wax the entire piece** with dark brown paste wax. Reattach hardware.

MOROCCAN TABLE
(PROJECT SHOWN ON PAGE 27)

- **This project is created with a vintage table.** Sand with *medium-grit sandpaper* and wipe clean. Apply *primer* with a 2-inch brush. Sand with *fine-grit sandpaper*. Wipe clean and paint entire table with two coats of red paint using a 2-inch brush.
- **Draw the design.** Work out the details with *paper* and *pencil* before transferring to the painted tabletop. On *tracing paper*, draw a circle with a *compass* to equal the same size as the center field. Tape tracing paper to get the size you need.
- **Fold a quarter circle.** Fold the quarter circle into eighths, fold again in sixteenths to create folds for a symmetrical eight-point star.
- **Open up the paper back to the quarter circle.** Use the three center folds of your paper as the guidelines. Working clockwise, measure 2½ inches down from the first and third folds. Use a *straightedge* and draw a line from the first mark to the edge of the circle on the folds to the right and left. Repeat for the second mark to make one-quarter of the star. Measure ¾ inch down from the star outline to repeat this design. Measure ⅜ inch from this line to draw the lines for the inner field of the star design.
- **Open the paper** one fold to the half circle. Turn the paper over and trace the quarter star design. Open for one half of the star. Turn the paper over and trace the half star to complete the whole star.
- **To transfer the design** to the tabletop, turn the drawing over, pencil side down. Center the circle with the center of the table. Transfer the design.

- **To add the leaf design** to the outside points of the star, place a piece of tracing paper over one of the points. Make a drawing of the leaf on each side. Trace leaves at each point of the star on the tabletop. As an alternative, make a stencil for the leaf design. **See page 285 for stencil directions.**
- **Mask off lines** with *painter's tape* to keep lines neat. With an artist's brush, paint the inner star with white acrylic paint. Rub the paint on the field with a brush to create a mottled effect that allows some of the amber to show through. Allow to dry. Mask off lines again to keep outlines neat. Paint the outer star with aqua acrylic paint, leaving the ⅜-inch band of amber between the white center field and the aqua star.
- **Mix crimson** and blue for purple. If necessary, add a touch of black to shade or a touch of white to tint. Or use a tube of purple artist's paint. Paint the leaves with a watercolor brush.
- **While the colors are drying,** create the inner design on the tracing paper star. Set the compass at ¼ inch and make a ½-inch circle at the center point. From the top (north) point of the star, draw a line to the bottom (south) point with a ruler and pencil. Repeat from the left.
- **Place a piece of tracing paper** over the drawing, concentrating on the top (north) point and centerline. Sketch the red petal design, keeping the top point at the center. Curve the line down and out to the left. Curve sharply down to connect with the ½-inch circle at the center. Curve the right side up, out, and down; then curve sharply into two upper petals.

- **At the middle of the upper petals,** draw an apostrophe shape pointing into the star point to the right of the design. The shape should be into, but not flush with, the edge.
- **When you are satisfied with the shape,** trace the back side with a *No. 2 lead pencil.* Turn the paper over and line up the design with one of the center lines on the original drawing. Trace this design on each line—north, south, east, and west.
- **Trace this design onto** the white center field and paint the petals with red latex paint, making the windmill design. Keep the outline neat.
- **Mix a dab of black** with blue acrylic paint to make dark blue. Paint the apostrophes with a watercolor brush. Allow the top to dry thoroughly.
- **Following crackle glaze directions,** apply one coat to table base and tabletop border. When these are dry, apply one coat of red paint, brushing in one direction. Allow to dry.
- **Protect the finish** with one coat of satin-finish polyurethane. Let it dry.
- **After the surface has dried,** mix burnt umber and black in a 3 to 1 ratio, so that the mixture appears more brown than black. Slightly thin the mixture with mineral spirits, and brush the mixture over the entire table. Wipe off excess, letting the pigment accumulate in carvings, grooves, cracks, and imperfections for a rustic look. Allow to dry. Finish with a coat of satin-finish polyurethane, allowing to dry. Sand with fine-grit sandpaper. Wipe with a damp rag. Apply the second coat of polyurethane.

PARISIAN SKETCHBOOK BEDROOM

SKILL LEVEL

Advanced

TIME

4 days

SUPPLIES

- All-purpose cleaner
- Fine- and medium-grit sandpaper
- Tack cloth
- Stain-blocking primer
- 2-inch paintbrush
- Paper
- Scissors
- Flat sponges
- No. 2 lead pencil
- White flat latex paint
- Yellow green, pink, lilac, blue, black acrylic latex paint
- Crafts knife
- Artist's round brush
- Matte-finish polyurethane

PARISIAN SKETCHBOOK BEDROOM
(PROJECT SHOWN ON PAGE 160–161)

- **This project is based on a** 1940s-style bed and dresser. Clean both pieces with a diluted all-purpose cleaner. Sand with fine-grit sandpaper, and wipe with a tack cloth. Apply a coat of stain-blocking primer/sealer. Allow to dry. Base-coat all pieces with flat white latex paint.

- **Dresser.** Choose a diamond size based on the size and scale of the dresser, referring to the photograph for scale. Cut a paper template of the diamond shape and trace it onto a sponge. Cut out the shape. Practice sponging the diamond on scrap paper. With a No. 2 lead pencil, lightly draw a line down the center of the dresser. Begin sponging at the top drawer, centered over the pencil line. Continue to sponge down the center line of the dresser. Using the photo as a guide, continue the process of sponging, using the additional colors and leaving a space between diamonds. Paint remaining areas of dresser as shown in photo.

- **Cut out stylized flowers from sponges** with a crafts knife. Dip the sponge into pink paint. Sponge the top of the arch on the dresser top. Allow to dry.

- **Lightly sketch the Eiffel Tower,** squiggles, and words in pencil. Using an artist's round brush, paint with black paint.

- **Bed.** Use the same supplies and techniques as for the dresser. Measure and mark the center of the headboard with a pencil. Make a diamond-shape sponge and, referring to the photograph, begin sponging down the center. Sponge along both sides, leaving space between the diamonds.

- **Sponge the flowers on the footboard** and on the center of the headboard. Paint solid colors as shown in photo on the headboard and footboard of the bed. Lightly sketch and paint details, following the instructions for the dresser.

- **Seal all pieces** with two coats of matte-finish polyurethane.

**COWBOY HEAVEN
DRESSER
SKILL LEVEL**
Intermediate
TIME
3 days
SUPPLIES
- Fine-grit sandpaper
- Tack cloth
- Crackle medium
- 6-inch foam roller
and covers
- Foam brush
- Black and off-white
flat or satin latex paint
- 1 quart latex
glazing liquid
- Burnt umber
acrylic paint
- Paint trays
- Lint-free rags
- Clear, matte-finish
acrylic spray finish

COWBOY HEAVEN DRESSER
(PROJECT SHOWN ON PAGE 168)

- **This project uses a previously painted dresser.** Remove the drawers from the dresser and remove the drawer pulls. Sand all dresser surfaces with fine-grit sandpaper; wipe with a tack cloth.
- **Apply a coat of crackle sizing** to the dresser with the foam roller, making sure not to drip the medium. Use a foam brush for hard-to-reach places. Let the medium dry until no longer tacky to the touch. Apply a second coat of crackle medium. Discard the roller cover. When the second coat is no longer tacky (1 to 2 hours), pour a generous amount of off-white paint in the roller tray. Saturate foam roller with paint and apply a heavy layer to the dresser top.
- **Roll in one direction** to the edge of the dresser in one smooth motion. Add more paint to the roller and roll a second roller width, making sure the edges line up but do not overlap. (Rolling over previously painted areas will lift the paint from them, interfering with the crackling process.) Repeat this process for the sides and front of the dresser. Allow to dry for 24 hours. Paint will crackle on its own. Repeat the crackling process on the drawer fronts, except for where the black paint is applied. (Here as the center ovals.) The black paint can be applied with a roller or a small foam brush if it is narrower.

- **After the dresser and drawers have dried** for at least 24 hours, mix 1 cup of the glazing liquid with 1 tablespoon of burnt umber paint. Pour the mixture into a clean roller pan. Roll the mixture onto a small section of the top of the dresser. Blot with a clean rag to remove some of the glaze. Do not blot the edges of the wet glaze; you must roll the next section of glaze next to this wet edge and then begin blotting the seam to blend the two sections so that no roller line is apparent. Continue this process on the entire piece. Allow to dry for about 8 hours. Spray with two coats of clear matte sealant for protection. Allow to dry completely between coats.

ROMANTIC WHITE BEDROOM

SKILL LEVEL

Beginner

TIME

2 to 3 days

SUPPLIES

- General purpose cleaner
- Lint-free rags
- White semigloss latex paint
- Raw umber artist's acrylic paint
- Clear paste wax

FOLK ART TRAY TABLE

SKILL LEVEL

Intermediate

TIME

2 days

SUPPLIES

- Olive decorative paint
- 2-inch paintbrush
- Bronze and gray decorative metallic glaze
- Color-washing brush
- Cheesecloth
- Clear, matte-finish spray sealant

ROMANTIC WHITE BEDROOM
(PROJECT SHOWN ON PAGE 134)

■ **This project refreshes** previously antiqued vintage furniture without stripping. The directions also can be used to renew previously painted furniture. To refresh antiqued furniture that looks worn or discolored, clean with a general purpose cleaner. Allow to dry.

■ **Thin semigloss latex paint** in a 1-to-1 ratio with water. Rag over the surfaces with a soft, lint-free rag. Allow to dry. Paint details with interior semigloss paint. Allow to dry. Thin raw umber artist's acrylic paint and rub it into recessed areas for an antiqued effect. Wipe away excess with a clean rag. Finish with a coat of clear paste wax or water-based polyurethane.

■ **Add unfinished pieces to blend** with the refreshed antiqued pieces. Sand and prime the bookcase, or other unfinished piece, and paint with satin latex paint.

FOLK ART TRAY TABLE
(PROJECT SHOWN ON PAGE 147)

■ **This is an ideal project to revive** an aged wooden or metal tray table. Sand peeling paint with a *fine-grit sandpaper*, if painted, and wipe with *tack cloths*. Apply appropriate *wood or metal primer* before applying the base coat.

■ **When the primer is dry,** brush on the olive base coat and let dry 4–6 hours. When the top of the tray is completely dry, turn over and paint underneath with the olive base coat and allow to dry. If painting a metal tray, expect quicker drying time than a wood tray. (An unfinished wood tray will need a second coat.)

■ **Pour about 1 cup** of the bronze metallic glaze into a plastic container. Dip the end of a color-washing brush into the glaze and apply to the top of the tray, using quick X-style strokes. While the glaze is wet, dab with dry cheesecloth to create a mottled effect. Allow to dry about 3 to 4 hours; turn the tray over, and repeat on the underside of the tray. Allow to dry.

■ **Pour about 1 cup** of gray metallic glaze into a *plastic container*. Brush on the gray glaze with quick X-style strokes. Dab with dry cheesecloth. Let dry 4 to 5 hours; repeat on the underside of the tray. Let the tray dry.

■ **Apply two coats of spray sealant.** Allow sealant to dry after each coat.

BOLD & BRIGHT DINING CHAIRS

SKILL LEVEL

Beginner

TIME

2 days

SUPPLIES

- Sandpaper
- Tack cloth
- 2-inch paintbrush
- Red, dark yellow, blue wood stains
- 2-inch nylon bristle paintbrush
- Matte-finish top coat

BOLD & BRIGHT DINING CHAIRS
(PROJECT SHOWN ON PAGES 180–181)

- **This project uses unfinished wood chairs.**
Sand the wood and remove the sanding dust with a tack cloth. Brush on one coat of stain in the desired color. Let the stain dry for 2 hours. (Depending on temperature and humidity, allow extra drying time.) Apply a second coat; let the finish dry. Brush on a matte-finish top coat; allow the finish to dry.

- **Sand lightly, remove the sanding dust with a tack cloth,** and apply a second coat of finish. This project mixes chairs finished with three different colors of translucent stain. If you prefer, choose one or two colors from the list or create your own combinations.

INTERLOCKING SQUARES
(PROJECT SHOWN ON PAGE 215)
(STENCIL PATTERN ON PAGE 314)

SKILL LEVEL

Beginner

TIME

2 days

SUPPLIES (IN ADDITION TO THE BASIC SUPPLY LIST ON PAGES 8–9)

- 3 colors of water-based porch paint
- Medium-size brush
- Blue painter's tape
- Water-based sealer

- **The interlocking squares stencil pattern** works well for porch floors because of its simplicity.
- **As a first step,** paint the porch floor with water-based porch paint. Allow to thoroughly dry. Mask a 12-inch border with blue painter's tape. With the second shade of water-based paint, paint around the porch perimeter for the impression of an area rug. Place the stencil randomly, reminiscent of old linoleum patterns. Using water-based floor paint, stencil with a medium-size brush in a pouncing motion. Apply the overlay the same way. Allow to dry. Seal with a water-based sealer for durability.

COWBOY HEAVEN ARMOIRE

SKILL LEVEL

Beginner

TIME

1 day

SUPPLIES

- Images to photocopy and decoupage
- Foam paintbrush
- Decoupage medium

RIBBONS AND ROSES GIRL'S LAMP

SKILL LEVEL

Intermediate

TIME

1 day

SUPPLIES

- 1 wooden lamp painted white
- 1-inch plain white shade
- Blue painter's tape
- Medium pink, light bright green, violet, white acrylic paints
- 1-inch flat brush
- Liner brush
- Unused pencil eraser end

COWBOY HEAVEN ARMOIRE
(PROJECT SHOWN ON PAGE 169)

- **This project uses a painted armoire** with paneled doors. Images can be found in art books, such as those about Frederic Remington. Size images to fit the panels. Apply a generous coat of decoupage medium to a door panel with a foam paintbrush. Carefully place the image on the panel, making sure there are no wrinkles. Gently smooth out any bubbles. Allow to dry (about ½ hour). Apply a coat of decoupage medium on top of the image.
- **Continue adding layers of decoupage medium** until you can no longer feel the edge of the photocopied image; it may take four to five coats. Allow to dry completely between each coat.

RIBBONS AND ROSES GIRL'S LAMP
(ROSE AND HEART STENCIL PATTERN ON PAGE 150–151)

- **Divide the shade into four equal sections,** using low-tack painter's tape and securing the tape firmly. Paint the shade medium pink with the 1-inch flat brush. Remove the tape. Allow to dry. Use the liner brush to outline each pink section with light bright green. Dip the eraser end of a pencil into violet paint to dot the white stripes of the shade.
- **Divide the lamp stem into four sections.** Paint the first section green and white checks, using a 1-inch brush.
- **Draw patterns on the lamp stem.** Paint the first section green and white checks with a 1-inch brush. Paint stripes on the second section using a 1-inch brush and violet paint; use a liner brush to add lines of bright light green, and add pink dots with a pencil eraser end. Paint the third lamp stem section the same as the surround on the armoire, using pink rosebuds and violet dimensional hearts. Base coat the fourth section pink; add vines and leaves with the liner brush and light bright green. Paint the base of the lamp light bright green; use a pencil eraser end and white paint to make dots in the green.

RIBBONS AND ROSES GIRL'S ARMOIRE

SKILL LEVEL

Intermediate

TIME

3 to 4 days

SUPPLIES

- Primer
- Pure white, light pink, medium pink, light bright green, blue, violet latex paint (quart size)
- 1½-inch, 3-inch latex brushes
- Pencil
- Ruler
- Tracing paper, carbon paper
- ½-inch flat, No. 2 small round liner artist's brushes
- Unused pencil eraser end
- Clear matte sealant

RIBBONS AND ROSES GIRL'S ARMOIRE
(PROJECT SHOWN ON PAGES 150–151)
(STENCIL PATTERN ON PAGE 316)

- **Prime and base-coat unfinished armoire with pure white.** Paint the bottom portion of the crown molding and the beveled edges of the door panels pink. With a pencil and a ruler, lightly mark 6-inch squares on the sides of the armoire. Paint every other square pink to form a check pattern. Allow to dry.

- **Paint the outer edges of the doors and the top of the crown molding blue.** Following the same procedure, paint them with the violet paint. Paint crown molding and door details in blue and light bright green.

- **Size stencil patterns** to fit your furniture piece. The lattice ribbon pattern is used for the door panels, and the roses and hearts are used on the panel surrounds. Trace the patterns onto tracing paper, and transfer the patterns onto the projects with carbon paper and a pencil. Transfer the pattern using violet paint, a ½-inch flat brush, and a small round brush. Outline the ribbons using a liner brush. Where the ribbon folds over itself, paint brush strokes to add dimension. Paint roses light pink, using a small round brush. Shade with medium pink, using a liner brush. Dot violet paint as heart-shaped accents around the roses using an unused pencil eraser end. Paint leaves green.

- **Seal with a coat of clear matte sealant.**

OLD-FASHIONED GIRL'S ROOM

SKILL LEVEL

Beginner

TIME

4–5 days

SUPPLIES

- Medium- and fine-grit sandpaper
- Tack cloth
- Stain-blocking primer
- Soft green, pink, pale yellow, white acrylic paints
- 2-inch paintbrush
- Clear, satin-finish polyurethane
- Glass pulls

OLD-FASHIONED GIRL'S ROOM
(PROJECT SHOWN ON PAGES 154–156)

- **This project brightens and updates** mismatched pieces of vintage furniture. If you purchase vintage or flea market furniture for such a project, shop for pieces with interesting shapes and detailing, such as the tall chest and dressing table. Don't be deterred by dark stains or chipped paint. With proper preparation, most pieces can be revived for a youthful look.

- **Choose colors that coordinate with** existing wall colors or fabrics in the room. An heirloom quilt provides the inspiration for this room. Remove hardware from chests and vanities. Sand first with medium- and then fine-grit sandpaper. Remove sanding dust with a tack cloth. Prime all surfaces with stain-blocking primer sealer, and allow the paint to dry thoroughly.

- **Paint the surface colors** as shown. Brush on a base coat with long smooth strokes to ensure a smooth finish. Recoat if necessary, allowing drying time between the coats. (Warm, dry days are ideal for painting. The more time between coats, the more durable the finish.) When the base coat is dry, paint the tops of each piece.

- **After each piece is completely dry,** seal with nonyellowing, satin-finish, clear polyurethane. Allow to dry. Reattach original hardware or affix new pulls.

DINO AND MORE

SKILL LEVEL

Intermediate

TIME

3 days

SUPPLIES

- Red, pale green, navy, lilac, yellow, orange acrylic latex paints
- 2-inch tapered brush
- Small tube of forest green crafts paint
- Black paint marker
- Fine-grit sandpaper
- Tack cloth
- White candle for waxing
- Nonyellowing, matte-finish polyurethane
- Stencil
- Spray adhesive
- Small stencil brushes

DINO AND MORE

(PROJECT SHOWN ON PAGE 171)
(STENCIL PATTERN ON PAGE 316)

- **These projects use stock unfinished furniture.** All pieces are sanded and primed before painting.
- **Paint the headboard pale green.** Allow to dry. With a 2-inch tapered brush paint multicolored horizontal waves, referring to the photo on page 171. Waves don't have to be opaque; allow some of the pale green to show through. Add narrow forest green waves; detail them with vertical dashes using a black paint marker. Allow to dry. Lightly sand the headboard with fine sandpaper. Wipe clean with a tack cloth. Seal with nonyellowing matte finish polyurethane.
- **Paint the toy chest** with one coat of pale green. Allow to dry. Wax the edges. Paint the inside navy, the lid red, the front orange, and the front bottom blue, as shown. The sides remain pale green. Allow to dry. Lightly sand the chest, and wipe with a tack cloth.
- **Apply the dinosaur stencil** on the front center of the chest. Using repositionable spray stencil adhesive, stencil the dinosaur body lilac and the dinosaur spines red. Allow the paint to dry. Detail the dinosaur with a black paint marker and add hand-painted yellow spots. Allow to dry. Seal with matte-finish, nonyellowing polyurethane.
- **Paint the chairs** pale green. Allow to dry. Rub a candle onto the edges and in streaks, going with the grain of the wood. Do not wax the legs and spindles.

- **Brush a thin layer of navy paint** onto the chair seats. Brush a thin layer of orange on the slat across the top of the chair. Allow to dry. Sand with fine-grit sandpaper and wipe clean. Paint will sand easily from areas streaked with wax, revealing the green base. Detail the chair seats and slats with red and green paint. Allow to dry.
- **Paint the table pale green.** Allow to dry. Use the candle wax technique on the tabletop in the same manner as the chairs. Paint the top navy. Allow to dry. Sand with fine-grit sandpaper to remove some of the navy. Wipe with a tack cloth. Detail as shown. Add the stenciled dinosaur or a design of your own. **(See page 285 for stencil directions.)**

AROUND THE WORLD DRESSER

SKILL LEVEL

Intermediate

TIME

4–5 days

SUPPLIES

- Fine-grit sandpaper
- Tack cloth
- White shellac primer
- 2-inch paintbrush
- Brick red exterior flat latex paint
- Commercial stencils
- Spray adhesive
- White artist's acrylic paint
- Round stencil brush
- Walnut one-step stain and sealer

AROUND THE WORLD DRESSER
(PROJECT SHOWN ON PAGE 171)

■ **This project uses a vintage dresser.** Remove the pulls and sand the dresser surface with fine-grit sandpaper. Wipe with a tack cloth. Prime the dresser with white shellac. Allow to dry. Brush on two coats of red latex paint with a 2-inch paint brush. Allow to dry between coats.

■ **Position the stencils** with repositionable spray adhesive. Use white artist's acrylic paint and a round stencil brush to stencil the design. The paint will appear bright. Allow the stencil paint to dry, then achieve an aged look by wiping the chest and pulls with one-step stain sealer. Attach pulls when the finish is dry.

DOG AND CAT NURSERY SKILL LEVEL

Intermediate

TIME

4 days

SUPPLIES

- Commercial stencils
- Red, green, aqua, blue, black satin finish latex paint (1 quart each)
- Glaze medium
- Sea sponges
- Yellow satin finish latex paint (2 quarts)
- 2-inch brush

BUNNY NURSERY SKILL LEVEL

Intermediate

TIME

5 days

SUPPLIES

- Self-adhesive paper
- Light, medium, dark green satin finish latex paint (1 quart each)
- Pale pink, peach, hot pink, lavender, purple, black satin finish latex paint (1 quart each)
- Glaze medium
- Sea sponges

DOG AND CAT NURSERY STENCIL
(PROJECT SHOWN ON PAGES 166–167)

- Look for commercial stencils of cats and dogs at local crafts or hobby stores.
- **Start with white walls** for the background.
- **Measure the walls** and determine the placement of the stencils. Space the squares with the motif around the room. Using a *level with printed measurements* and a *pencil*, mark the placement of the squares. Stencil the border for each square with a *small stencil brush*.
- **When the border is dry,** tape the motifs—dog, cat, bone, and paw prints—in the center of each square. Dab a sea sponge in a tiny bit of glaze then into the paint color, blot and cover the area evenly with a blotting motion. Use one sea sponge for each color. After the motifs are dry, use a *small round artist's brush* to add details.
- **Allow squares with motifs** to dry completely. Above and below motifs, measure 6-inch-wide stripes and lightly draw guide lines. Mask off stripes with *blue painter's tape*. Loosely brush on yellow paint with a two-inch brush. Dip a sea sponge in glaze and blot over painted stripes to soften the effect.

BUNNY IN THE GARDEN NURSERY STENCIL
(PROJECT SHOWN ON PAGES 158–159)
(STENCIL PATTERN ON PAGE 313)

- For a pleasing placement of motifs, use *scissors* to cut out paper patterns of the stencils and tape to the wall before you begin. Determine the size of the fence pickets based on the size of the room. The pickets in this project measure 4 inches wide by 28 inches high. Cut fence pickets from self-adhesive paper. Position on the wall. Dab a sea sponge in glaze, then green paint. Sponge between the pickets to create the grass. When the glaze is dry, remove paper and hand-paint dark green nail details.
- **For vegetables,** tape patterns to the walls to determine positions using *blue painter's tape*. Hand-paint wavy lines for peas and vines. Tape stencil and stencil vegetables. For the soft, painterly effect of this project, dab a sea sponge in glaze, then hand-paint in a blotting motion over the stencil. When dry, paint loose green detail swirls with a *small artists brush*.
- **Outline the bunny by hand** with a *pencil*, copying the photographs. Loosely paint the outline with black paint and a small artists brush. (Practice first on *scrap paper* to be sure of the effect.) After all the motifs are painted, detailed, and dry, mix the background glaze using one part lavender paint, one part white paint, and two parts glaze in a *plastic container*. With a loose, freehand motion, brush the glaze mixture onto the wall with a *2-inch paintbrush*. Blend and soften with a sea sponge dipped in glaze. **(See page 285 for stencil directions.)**

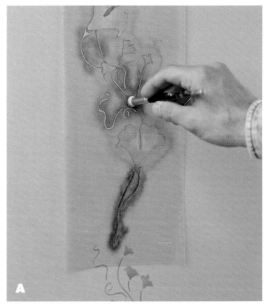

GINKGO COUNTRY LIVING ROOM

SKILL LEVEL

Intermediate

TIME

1½ days

SUPPLIES

- Yellow latex paint if repainting wall
- Ginkgo leaf commercial stencil with overlays
- Olive green, dark green, brown oil-based stencil paints
- Small stencil brushes

GINKGO COUNTRY LIVING ROOM STENCIL
(PROJECT SHOWN ON PAGES 108–109)

- **This project features stencil overlays,** which are used for more detailing. When you use commercial overlays, carefully follow the directions.

- **Always begin with Stencil A** and work alphabetically. After the first sheet is stenciled around the room, match the registration outlines and stencil second overlay (Stencil B). For best results, pay careful attention to stenciling around doorways.

- **Start at the top left hand side of the door frame.** (The leaves should point up from the woodwork.) Stencil down to the baseboard. Apply the second color to stems and areas to be shaded for a natural look. If the stencil run doesn't end in a complete pattern, choose where to end the stencil. Do not stencil half a leaf, for example; rather, stop at the most attractive point.

A Position first stencil. Apply one paint color to leaves. Apply the second paint color to the stems and areas to be shaded. Allow to dry.

B Line up second overlay with pattern on the wall. Stencil remaining details. Continue with additional overlays, if applicable. Stencil above the baseboard with leaves pointing down.

- **Wash the stencil.** To stencil the right side of the door frame, flip the stencil over and keep leaves pointing up from the frame.

FRENCH BLUE AND WHITE CHAIRS
SKILL LEVEL
Beginner
TIME
2 days
SUPPLIES
- White, four shades of blue low-luster satin finish latex paint
- Commercial stencil
- Stencil brush
- Lint-free rags

SWEDISH LINEN
SKILL LEVEL
Beginner
TIME
3 days
SUPPLIES
- White shellac primer
- Water-based glaze
- Blue acrylic paint
- 3-inch paintbrush
- Commercial stencil
- Clear, water-based, matte-finish sealer

FRENCH BLUE AND WHITE CHAIRS
(PROJECT SHOWN ON PAGE 195)

- **This project uses unfinished** dining chairs. Sand and prime the chairs before applying the base coat.
- **This project uses four varied** shades of blue paint. If you prefer, choose just one or two shades for your project.
- **Apply the first coat** of paint with a *2-inch paint brush*, choosing a different color for each chair. Let the paint dry on each chair for 6 to 8 hours. Apply a second coat; let the paint dry for 6 to 8 hours.
- **Measure the center point of the back panel of the chair,** and position the stencil, using repositionable *spray adhesive*. Choose a commercial stencil with a fleur-de-lis or a similar stylized motif. Pour 3 tablespoons of white paint into a plastic container. Dip the stencil brush into the paint, dab off excess on a rag, and firmly dab paint onto the opening of the stencil. Repeat the stenciling process for all chairs. Let the stenciled motif dry for 4 hours. Touch up chair paint as needed.

SWEDISH LINEN
(PROJECT SHOWN ON PAGE 196)

- **This project uses an unfinished desk, which has been primed** with white shellac primer. Use *fine-grit sandpaper* and sand a stained desk, wipe with *tack cloths*, and prime with the white shellac primer. Allow to dry. Tint water-based glaze with blue acrylic. To create a subtle linen effect, horizontally brush on glaze with a 3-inch paintbrush. Allow to dry. Brush second coat of glaze in the vertical direction. Use a commercial stencil to detail as shown.
- **Seal with a clear sealer** in a matte finish.

MONKEYS ON PATROL
SKILL LEVEL
Advanced
TIME
2 days
SUPPLIES
- Large piece of stencil plastic or acetate
- Pencil
- Crafts knife
- Graphite paper if needed
- Brown or tan acrylic paint
- Dark brown acrylic paint
- Small stencil brushes
- Red acrylic paint

MONKEYS ON PATROL STENCIL
(PROJECT SHOWN ON PAGES 148–149)
(STENCIL PATTERN ON PAGE 314)

- **Enlarge the stencil** to a scale appropriate to your room. Use an oversize copier at a copy center. Trace the monkey outline onto stencil plastic, a large piece of poster board, or acetate. Cut out the monkey outline with a crafts knife; label it Stencil A.

- **Trace the monkey details**. Details include eyes, hair, and toes. Make a stencil for the details by tracing over the pattern and enlarging. Trace details onto stencil material. Draw the outline of the monkey onto the stencil so you will know where to lay the stencil when you are ready. Cut out the details only. Label this Stencil B. Make a stencil for the ball. Cut out.

A Place Stencil A, the monkey shape, onto the wall. Place it in a spot where the monkey will appear to be hanging from a vine. (The vine will be added later.)

- **Stencil this first overlay** in solid medium brown or tan paint using a small stencil brush.

B Use darker brown to shade outline of monkey.

C After allowing outline to dry, place Stencil B on top, lining it up so all the details are positioned correctly. Stencil these details in a dark brown.

- **Stencil the red ball** in the monkey's paw.

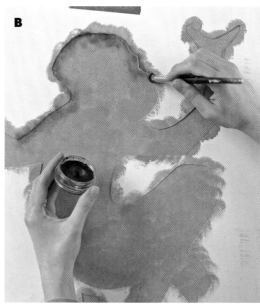

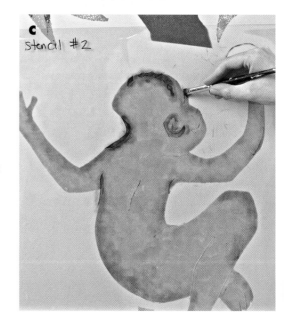

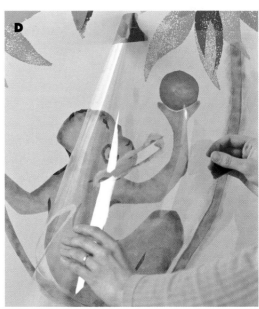

VINES AND FRONDS
SKILL LEVEL
Intermediate
TIME
1½ days
SUPPLIES
- Stencil plastic or acetate
- Medium and dark values of brown stencil paints
- Plate or paint tray
- Compressed sponge for leaves
- Scissors
- Pen
- Two medium values of green
- Scrap board
- One dark value of green
- Blue painter's tape
- Acetate

VINES AND PALM FRONDS
(PROJECT SHOWN ON PAGES **148–149**)
(STENCIL PATTERN ON PAGE **315**)

■ **For the palm fronds and branches,** begin by drawing branch shapes onto a large piece of stencil plastic. Use simple curved shapes and determine the length of branches you would like to use for the particular space, making several sizes, with ends curved in different directions.

■ **Stencil these branches** into place with brown paint, leaving enough room for leaves on each side of the branches. Use a pen to trace leaf shapes onto the compressed sponge and cut out with scissors. Enlarge leaf shapes with water and wring out.

A Pour a medium green paint color into a plate or paint tray. Dip sponge into paint and blot onto a piece of scrap board.

■ **Sponge the fronds along the branches,** overlapping and moving in slightly different directions. Make them appear as they would in a natural jungle setting.

B Sponge second medium green color for additional leaves to work with the wall space.

C Add dark green accents. Repeat for all branches.

D At this point, stencil monkey (see page 314). To add vine for monkey, tape a large piece of acetate to the wall, over the monkey. Draw a vine onto the acetate placed to appear as if the monkey were perched on it. Draw so the vine disappears into the palm branches or the ceiling. Cut out vines. Stencil in a medium to dark brown with darker brown shadows.

PORCH WITH PIZZAZZ
SKILL LEVEL
Intermediate
TIME
3 to 4 days
SUPPLIES
- Commercial concrete etcher
- Xylene (for cleaning brushes)
- Silicon acrylic Concrete stain in light buff, brick red, seafoam green, and Caribbean blue
- 2-inch-wide masking tape
- 4-inch roller frame and covers
- Four 14×16-inch sheets of acetate
- Crafts knife
- Spray adhesive
- Pencil
- Aluminum plate
- 2-inch paintbrush
- 5 foam plates
- Artist's liner brush (10/0 size)

PORCH WITH PIZZAZZ
(PROJECT SHOWN ON PAGES **224–225**)
(STENCIL PATTERNS ON PAGE **317**)

Note: The project was designed for a concrete porch; however, the motifs translate to wood porches. If you work on concrete, scrape and pressure wash it to remove debris. Acid-wash concrete with a commercial concrete etcher according to manufacturer's directions, using a push broom and watering can. FOLLOW ALL SAFETY PRECAUTIONS. Wear safety goggles and cover plantings with plastic. Let the clean concrete dry for 72 hours.

- **Paint the entire porch** light buff according to the manufacturer's directions. If you paint only roses, continue with the following directions. If you paint the rug motif, as shown in the featured project, tape off the outer perimeter of the desired rug size now. Do not paint in the taped off area. Let dry 24 hours. To continue with the rug, remove the tape and then tape off a 5-inch border; paint the border blue. Let dry 24 hours and tape off the center of the rug. Paint it seafoam green. Clean rollers.

- **Enlarge or reduce stencil** patterns to fit the space. For sizing, first photocopy stencils from this book and size up or down on a photocopier.

- **Cut out stencils with stencil** plastic and a crafts knife. The rose is made with an outline stencil and an overlay for the details. See monkey stencil project, page 304, for more information on tracing, cutting, and working with detail overlays.

- **Randomly lay out the solid rose stencil** on the porch floor, marking the outline with a pencil to be sure of placement. Spray stencil adhesive to the back of the stencil and place the stencil over the pencil outline. Pour brick red paint into an aluminum plate. With a 2-inch paintbrush, fill in with brick red paint, working quickly. Do not over brush. Dry 24 hours.

- **Place the stencil** for the rose details over the solid painted rose. Use spray adhesive to hold in place. Mix one part brick red and one part light buff in a foam plate. Pour light buff into a second foam plate. With an artist's liner brush, first dip the brush into a generous amount of the mixed paint, then directly into the solid buff paint. Without mixing paints, swipe along the pierced stencil's opening. Reapply paints to brush as needed, alternating the colors.

- **To add definition to each rose,** dip the liner brush into the mixed paint and loosely trace a shadow line of paint around the stenciled line and intermittently around the perimeter.

- **For leaves,** make the solid leaf stencil. Trace the stencil into varying positions around the roses, penciling in two or three leaves per rose. Fill in solid leaf stencil with seafoam green; dry 24 hours. Mix equal amounts of seafoam green and light buff and stencil the leaf overlay over the solid leaves. Dry 24 hours. For the rug, make the star stencil and stencil randomly in light buff on the seafoam background. Use an artist's brush to paint a wavy seafoam green line on the Caribbean blue rug border. Randomly add light buff dots between the wavy lines.

FRESH-AIR WICKER CHAIR

SKILL LEVEL

Beginner

TIME

2 days

SUPPLIES

- Liquid deglosser
- Dark green acrylic spray paint
- Walnut stain
- Blowdryer
- Sponge
- 2-inch paintbrush

FRESH-AIR WICKER CHAIR

(PROJECT SHOWN ON PAGE 230)

■ **This project is based on a painted wicker chair.** Do this messy project outdoors, using drop cloths to protect the grass or patio. Clean and degloss the chair with deglosser so paint will adhere. Allow to dry.

■ **Spray with green paint** and allow to dry for at least 1 hour. Brush stain over the painted finish. To get stain into the weave of the wicker, brush on liberally. Use a hair dryer set on cool to blow into the crevices. Wipe the stain off the high surfaces with a sponge. Brush out drips with a paintbrush.

FRESH-AIR END TABLE

(PROJECT SHOWN ON PAGE 230)

SKILL LEVEL

Beginner

TIME

½ day

SUPPLIES

- Tape measure
- Embossed wallpaper
- Scissors
- Wallpaper paste
- White satin-finish spray paint
- Walnut stain
- Oil-based faux finishing glaze
- Lint-free rags

■ **Measure the top of the table** and cut the wallpaper to fit. Use wallpaper paste and glue paper to the top of the table. Allow to dry. Spray the piece white. Allow to dry. Use a rag and wipe with a stain mixed with glaze to enhance detailing and embossing.

CHAIRS WITH PERSONALITY

SKILL LEVEL
Beginner
TIME
2 to 3 days
SUPPLIES
- Fine-grit sandpaper
- Primer
- Pale shades of
yellow, blue, green,
purple latex paints
- Small paintbrush
- Sealer

ADIRONDACK REVIEW
BENCH

SKILL LEVEL
Beginner
TIME
1 day
SUPPLIES
- Tinted primer
- Medium green,
dark green semigloss
paint suitable for
outdoor use
- Small paintbrush
- Sealer

CHAIRS WITH PERSONALITY
(PROJECT SHOWN ON PAGE **228**)

- **This project is based on matching rockers.** Work out your color combinations before beginning the project. Sand and prime the chairs. Paint the body of each chair one color with three other colors used for accents. Seal with an exterior sealer if rocker will be used outdoors.

ADIRONDACK REVIEW
COLOR-BLOCK CHAIRS

SKILL LEVEL
Beginner
TIME
2 days
SUPPLIES
- Tinted primer
- Two shades of green
semigloss paint
suitable for outdoor
use
- Small paintbrush
- Sealer

ADIRONDACK REVIEW BENCH

- **This project uses an unfinished bench** primed with tinted primer. This color scheme uses two shades of green paint suitable for exterior use. Tinted primer used under yellows, yellow-greens, and oranges provides better base color. Otherwise, these colors, which contain smaller amounts of pigment, would require additional coats of paint for coverage. Seal with exterior sealer.

ADIRONDACK REVIEW COLOR-BLOCK CHAIRS

- **This project, like the Adirondack bench,** is first primed with a tinted primer. Alternate color schemes that work well for these Adirondack chairs are shades of blue or crisp white plus a primary color. Seal with exterior sealer

PORCH WITH PUNCH BENCH

SKILL LEVEL

Intermediate

TIME

3 to 4 days

SUPPLIES

- Black, violet, olive green, yellow latex enamel paint
- 2-inch paintbrush
- Commercial stencil
- Dark yellow, burnt umber, dark green, brick red, red acrylic paints
- ½-inch flat artist's brush, small round, liner brush
- Blue painter's tape
- Straightedge
- Matte spray sealant

PORCH WITH PUNCH BENCH
(PROJECT SHOWN ON PAGES 226–227)

- **Prime if the bench is unfinished.** Base-coat the following areas using a 2-inch paintbrush: panels, yellow; panel insets and upper stiles, violet; back and lower stiles, olive green; and arms, seat, feet, and apron panels of the bottom section, black. After base-coating these areas and allowing them to dry, use a commercial stencil to add a cherry pattern or other motifs on the yellow panels.

- **Paint the stems** with the liner brush and burnt umber. Paint the leaves with a mix of dark yellow and dark green, using the ½-inch flat brush. Don't completely mix the two colors together, but leave some of the leaves with yellow areas and others with darker green areas. Paint the cherries, first with the dark yellow, then add red or brick red. Allow some of the yellow to peek through—especially in the center as a highlight. Add veins to the leaves and connect the cherries to the branches with burnt umber.

- **Make the seat pattern** marking off 3-inch sections across the front and back of the bench seat and using a straightedge to form diamonds. Mask diamond shapes and paint them olive green. Allow to dry and spray with two coats of matte sealant.

PORCH WITH PUNCH CHAIRS
(PROJECT SHOWN ON PAGE 226)

SKILL LEVEL

Beginner

TIME

1 day

SUPPLIES

- Fine-grit sandpaper
- Tack cloth
- Blue painter's tape
- Dark gray, bright green, bright blue latex stain
- 1-inch paint brushes
- Matte latex sealant

- **Sand the chairs with sandpaper** and wipe with tack cloth. Tape off the sections to be stained bright green. Apply the stain with a 1-inch paintbrush and allow it to penetrate the wood. Wipe with a clean cloth. Remove tape. Tape off sections to stain blue. Apply as with the green stain. Repeat the process, using the dark gray stain. Allow to dry. Seal with two coats of matte latex sealant.

GREEN FOLDING CHAIR
SKILL LEVEL
Beginner
TIME
1 day
SUPPLIES
- Medium green, bright green, orange, golden yellow, black, white flat interior latex paint
- Small paintbrushes
- ½-inch artist's brush
- Polyurethane satin finish

RED FOLDING CHAIR
SKILL LEVEL
Beginner
TIME
1 day
SUPPLIES
- Red, ochre flat interior latex paint
- Small paintbrushes
- ½-inch artist's brush
- Satin-finish polyurethane

FUN & FUNKY CAFE TABLE
SKILL LEVEL
Beginner
TIME
2 to 3 days
SUPPLIES
- Flat interior latex paint in bright colors: blue, red, orange, yellow, black, white
- ½-inch artist's brush
- Small artist's brush
- Satin-finish polyurethane

GREEN FOLDING CHAIR
(PROJECT SHOWN ON PAGE 229)
- **This project uses stained folding chairs.** Lightly sand the chairs, and apply one coat of *stain-blocking primer*. Let dry 1 hour. With a *pencil*, lightly draw the designs onto the seats and backs. Fill in with paint, using a ½-inch artist's brush and short, random strokes to create a mottled effect. Mix the two greens in small amounts to create color variations. Paint the sun and moon face. Let dry for 1 hour. Using an artist's brush, paint the eyes and mouth of the sun and moon face. Paint the framework of the chairs black. Allow to dry. Apply three coats of polyurethane. Allow to dry completely between each coat.

RED FOLDING CHAIR
(PROJECT SHOWN ON PAGE 229)
- **Lightly sand the seat and back** of stained folding chairs. Apply one coat of *stain-blocking primer*. Let dry 1 hour. Paint entire chair red. Let dry 2 hours. Draw the design with white chalk and fill in with primer. Let dry 1 hour. Fill in design with ochre. Let dry 2 hours. Apply three coats of polyurethane to finish. Allow to dry completely between each coat.

FUN & FUNKY ROUND CAFE TABLE
(PROJECT SHOWN ON PAGE 229)
- **This project is constructed with an unfinished tabletop** and an existing table base. Sand lightly and apply two coats of *primer*. Compose design on paper and transfer to tabletop. Lightly draw the design onto the tabletop with a *lead pencil*. Apply blue paint with a ½-inch artist's brush, using short, multidirectional strokes to create a mottled effect.
- **Repeat with the** yellow, orange, and red paints. Paint in the center with white paint. Let dry for 2 hours.
- **Outline all the shapes** with black paint, using a small artist's brush. Let dry 4 hours. Apply three coats of polyurethane, allowing each coat to dry for 2 hours.

DIRECTOR'S CHAIR
SKILL LEVEL
Beginner
TIME
1 day
SUPPLIES
- White chalk
- Gold, pale green flat interior latex paint
- ½-inch artist's brush

FRESH-AIR PORCH SWING
SKILL LEVEL
Intermediate
TIME
2 days
SUPPLIES
- Drapery finials
- Construction adhesive
- Victorian scroll
- Wood screws
- Acorn finials made for fence posts
- Walnut oil-based stain
- Small paintbrush
- White rust-preventing spray paint
- Sandpaper

DIRECTOR'S CHAIR
(PROJECT SHOWN ON PAGE 229)
- **This project uses a director's chair with dark fabric seat and back.** Remove the fabric from the chair, and lay it out on a table covered with a *drop cloth*. Lightly sketch the design onto the fabric with white chalk. Use an artist's brush and fill in with two coats of gold and green paint.

FRESH-AIR PORCH SWING
(PROJECT SHOWN ON PAGE 230)
- **This project is based on a 5-foot unfinished porch swing.** Assemble the swing and attach the large finials to the bottom. Predrill holes for wood screws at the top of the back of the swing. Attach the Victorian scrolls with wood screws and construction adhesive. Attach drapery finials to the outer edges of the horizontal slat across the top, aligning them with the finials at the bottom. Brush stain over the entire swing. Allow to dry.
- **Spray with the white paint.** When the paint is dry, sand the areas that would normally show some wear so that some of the brown stain is visible.

stencil patterns

DINING ROOM STENCIL,
PAGE 286

STAMPED LEAF GIRL'S ROOM,
PAGE 284

STAMPED LEAF GIRL'S ROOM,
PAGE 284

BUNNY IN THE GARDEN NURSERY STENCIL,
PAGE 301

MONKEYS ON PATROL BALL STENCIL, PAGE 304

MONKEYS ON PATROL STENCIL, PAGE 304
OUTLINE OVERLAY AND BASE, PAGE 304

**INTERLOCKING SQUARES STENCIL
WITH REGISTRATION MARKS, PAGE 295**

MONKEYS ON PATROL PALM FRONDS STENCIL,
PAGE 305

DINO STENCIL PATTERN PROJECT, PAGE 299

ROSE AND
HEART STENCIL
PATTERN
PROJECT FOR
LAMP SHADE
TECHNIQUE,
PAGE 296

RIBBON LATTICE STENCIL PATTERN PROJECT, PAGE 297

PORCH WITH PIZZAZZ STENCIL, PAGE 306

index

endless inspiration

for the style you love

Special low rates at www.bhg.com/order

Better Homes and Gardens.
America's leader for fresh, up-to-the-minute casual ... it's where decorating is made *easy!*

Country Home
Take a fresh look at country — unrehearsed, unfussy, understated.

TRADITIONAL HOME
Celebrate the grace and comfort of timeless design.

Midwest Living
Tour the heartland's most charming houses — soak up ideas for yours.

Hurry! This offer won't last!
Visit www.bhg.com/order today.